Redemption Through Divorce

How Christ works in Broken Hearts, Creating Hope and Healing

CINDY STEINBECK

ISBN-978-1-7337949-0-9

Manufactured in the United States of America

ALSO BY CINDY STEINBECK

The Vine Speaks
"I am the Vine; you are the branches."—Jesus

The Rock Speaks
"Who is a rock, except our God?"—David

Grapes of Grace
"Abide in me!"—Jesus

Acknowledgements

To the young couple on my winery patio, thank you for speaking God's word to me and uttering the beautiful words, "redemption through divorce." Cecy, Rachel, and Mary, thank you for your love and encouragement every step of my journey. Allen, thank you for your help with the Greek words and redemption concepts. Kristy, Marylou, and Lori, for reading and cheering me on. Geneace, for your wisdom and questions. Karen, for your faithful heart editing my work. Kathy, for photos, fun, and your friendship. To my children and grandchildren for the rich opportunity to play. You bring joy and healing to my heart.

Contents

	Acknowledgements	v
	Introduction	ix
	Greek Words and Greek Word Groups	xv
1	Divorced—A Statistic AND Human Being	1
2	God Hates Divorce—What? And Why?	13
3	God's Divorce—What? And Why?	25
4	Hope	33
5	Freedom	45
6	Intimacy	59
7	Redeemed From, Through AND For	73
8	Letting Go	83
9	Pain	93
10	Living Forgiveness	105
	CONCLUSION	115

Introduction

"I will never get divorced" were my confident words to my soon-to-be spouse. I remembered the divorces in our church as I was growing up all too vividly, and I was never going to be a divorce statistic. "Those divorced people," whom I loved, were a class unto themselves. Some left the church without a word of good-bye, others stayed. Within a few months of hearing about their divorce being final, I remember hearing comments about getting that person together with so and so—they would certainly be happy married to them.

The divorces I witnessed from afar stimulated many questions in my young mind, but the silence was deafening as I tried to understand why our friends divorced. I wanted to comprehend the end of their marriages, but I was a child and children don't ask adults questions about divorce. The only answer I received was "there is too much divorce in the church." Statistics, not broken human hearts, were discussed.

I observed the pain of our divorced friends and their silence as their hearts ached. I watched closely in great sorrow for them as others rolled their eyes when they talked about their divorce, behind their backs. The silence and the suffering led me to resolve with all certainty that I would never get divorced.

I am divorced; I am a divorce statistic, just like the people I remember with great love from my childhood. I got engaged in 1981; married in 1982; divorced in 2011. My marriage, my separation, and my divorce were painful and very painfully, silently, private. Being a divorce statistic, while something I never intended to be, also means that I am no longer living in the painful silence of a marriage filled with despair. I am learning to live life as a human being, no longer defined by being single, married or divorced.

As I speak my story, I more fully understand that my journey from despair to hope and healing, from silence to finding my voice, has brought hope to others. These next pages are filled with encouraging words of redemption, hope, and healing. I sit in the middle of my vineyard writing these words and praying they will bring hope to the divorced, the brokenhearted who have suffered or are suffering in silence and shame. My heart through these words is also for those who love someone who is divorced, for those who want to give encouragement and hope. My story is unique to me, but my engagement, my marriage, and my divorce have many similarities to the stories I've heard from men and women around the country. We need hope, we need a voice, we need mercy, and we need each other in this journey.

My journey took a beautiful turn when I chatted with a compassionate young couple visiting my winery tasting room on a cold January day. I joined them on my back covered patio, weary from a long flight home from Australia. Our rich conversation of the heart covered many topics, and they were wanted to hear my story. I shared that I had been married and had divorced my spouse. I felt the shame as shared that I never intended to divorce, but during our separation my spouse continued to blame everyone rather than take responsibility for his angry outbursts. I initiated my divorce.

I shared that I had begged God to grant me a humble heart and keep me kind and loving while facing the pain. "I deeply desired to walk a Godly walk, without bitterness or a desire for revenge" were words that flowed from my heart. I shared that I prayed for courage and hope for myself and for my former spouse.

I told this couple that as I have spoken around the country, I have heard many stories similar to mine. My journey from despair into hope and freedom, healing and restoration of my broken heart, was a testimony of God's work in me, and telling my story testified to God's work through me. Commenting on my words, this young man made a powerful statement, "God working redemption through divorce." Shortly thereafter the beautiful young couple went on their way.

"Redemption through divorce" rang in my heart like a call on an old house phone. A week later I called the young man to ask him why he framed his statement that way. First, he said, "I believe redemption is the theme of all Scripture." He continued, "my parents are divorced and somehow, they just cannot hear God's mercy for them. They think divorce is so bad they cannot hear or receive grace." That statement resonated with me! I knew Christ died for everyone, but what about my particular circumstance, for me, because I'm divorced?

I told him about my journey in the Scriptures under the theme of redemption through divorce. I told him about the Greek word groups I had found and the rich connections in the words redemption and divorce. I also shared that I had discovered that the words forgiveness, set free, and divorce are the same Greek words, apoluō and aphiemi. When I asked him if he knew the connections, he declared, "No, but I'm not surprised."

With excitement I continued to comb through the Scriptures, not as an expert in Greek but as a brokenhearted human being hungry for hope and healing. My brother, a minister, helped me access Greek sources as well as the Scripture references for my study.

My search of the Scriptures brought back painful memories of my search for the word "divorce" as I was going through the trauma of separation and eventually the end of my marriage. Reading Scripture verses on "divorce" in the midst of my crisis brought no hope. Looking for comfort in crisis I found only harsh words. My trapped mind raced with memories of the words, "God hates divorce" (Malachi 2:16). I had been told and believed that "divorce statistics are too high in the church, you have to save your marriage." I also heard, "you need to guard the institution of marriage at all cost." As I look back, I see clearly now what I wasn't aware of then. I was living in deep despair and depression. I was not living.

My new search of the Scriptures at a new season in life took on a different tone—one of excitement and hope. My new search also opened a lot of questions. How is it possible that the word "divorce" and "to set free" and "forgive" are the same Greek word? How is it that the associated words, redemption and deliver, have not been used as healing words in the midst of the crisis of divorce? Are words used intentionally against brokenhearted human beings torn apart by trauma in order to keep them bound in shame?

Additional discoveries and questions flowed. God divorced and sent Israel away with a certificate of divorce (Jeremiah 3:8). What can we learn from God's divorce? How does God work redemption through something he hates (Malachi 2:16)? Why are redemption, mercy, and forgiveness so hard to hear as a divorced human being? Can God really work redemption through divorce to bring hope and healing? Will he heal my broken heart?

Another troubling question lingered. Was it possible that I, a divorced woman, was simply seeking personal justification through the Holy Scriptures for the choice I made to end my marriage? The answer to this question is a resounding "no." I am not seeking justification, I'm seeking Jesus, hope, and healing. Fear of being a divorce statistic, self-doubt, and timidity have been swallowed up by God's call to be faithful to discuss divorce from the context of my painful journey. I have experienced redemption through divorce, and God continues to work redemption, hope, and healing in me. Here is the heart of God and bits of my heart, as I've experienced Christ creating hope and healing.

Greek Words and Greek Word Groups

The original Greek words provide a path for a deeper look into the various meanings of the words divorce, redemption, healing, and forgiveness. I have found great joy and comfort as I've focused my attention on the original language and God's work of redemption as it relates to divorce. These words have helped me answer the question, "How does God work, specifically, in my broken heart and the broken hearted who have experienced the pain and shame of divorce?"

I've placed the relevant Greek words, the associated Greek word groups, and some of the scriptural references below. As you read *Redemption Through Divorce,* please reference the words and the Scripture verses in which those words were used. Dive into these words, the associated scriptures, and discover God's work for and in you. (A Concordance to the Greek Testament Westcott and Hort, Tischendorf. Fifth edition, 1978.)

Apoluō is two words, apo and luō. Apo is a simple word meaning "from." Luō is to loosen, release, set free, destroy. Apoluō is translated: release, set free; send away; sendoff; divorce; forgive. Apoluō is used in the story of Jesus *freeing* a woman from a disease that kept her bound (Luke 13:12-16) as well as the story of Joseph wanting to *divorce* Mary quietly so she would not be put to shame (Matthew 1:18-19). Apoluō is used in Jesus' discussions of divorce (Matthew 5:31-32,19:3-9). Apoluō appears also in Jesus' parable to the servant's master taking pity and *canceling* his debt (Matthew 18:27), as well as in Jesus' words, *forgive* and you will be forgiven (Luke 6:37).

Lutrōsis means redemption, liberation, setting free. Zechariah, who had waited for redemption through Christ, prophesied in the presence of the infant Jesus, "he has come and has *redeemed* his people," (Luke 1:68). The author of the book of Hebrews wrote, "he entered once for all into the holy places, not by means of the blood of goats and calves but by means of his own blood, thus securing an eternal *redemption*," (Hebrews 9:12).

Apolutrōsis (apo and lutrōsis) is translated as setting free, deliverance, release, redemption, and liberation procured by the payment of a ransom. The apostle Paul makes use of this word as he proclaims Christ's work of redemption, "the righteousness of God through faith in Jesus Christ for all who believe. For there is no distinction: for all have sinned and fall short of the glory of God, are justified by his grace as a gift, through the *redemption* that is in Christ Jesus," (Romans 3:22-24; see also Romans 8:23, 1 Corinthians 1:30, Ephesians 1:7, 1:14, 4:30, Colossians 1:14).

Lutron indicates a means of release and a means of redeeming by ransom. Christ's sacrifice delivered people from the bondage of sin and death. Christ came to serve and to give his life as a *ransom* for many (Matthew 20:28, Mark 10:45). Lutron indicates both the sacrifice of the life of Christ as the only ransom acceptable to God as well as God's action of receiving his son's sacrifice.

Aphiemi means to give up a debt and forgive. Jesus calls us to pray in the Lord's Prayer, "*forgive* us our debts, as we also have forgiven our debtors" (Matthew 6:12). Aphiemi is translated forgive in Peter's question directed to Jesus, "how many times must I *forgive*?" (Matthew 18:21). Aphiemi is "giving up," as Christ, from the cross, "uttered a loud cry and *breathed his last*" (Mark 15:37). Aphiemi is translated as divorce in Paul's advice to the married, "if any woman has a husband who is an unbeliever, and he consents to live with her, she should not *divorce* him" (1 Corinthians 7:13).

CHAPTER 1

Divorced—A Statistic AND Human Being

I get a tight feeling in my stomach and shortness of breath when I sense a conversation in my winery tasting room heading toward the question, "what does your husband do in the business?" I've learned to pause and calmly say, "I'm not married." The person asking the question quickly says, "I'm sorry I didn't know" and moves on to other family stories. There was a day in the not-too-distant past when I fumbled with what words to say to my guest while internally, screaming, "I am divorced, a divorce statistic." I realize that the days where divorce defines me, in my own mind, are fading into my past.

While these words, divorce and divorced, no longer define me, they are important words to discuss. Divorce means a legal separation or legal dissolution of a marriage. If one is getting a divorce their divorce may be eminent, but it is a future event.

"I want a divorce" indicates a person's intent to initiate the legal process to end a marriage. He is divorced; she is divorced; they are divorced; I am divorced. Individuals who have been married and are now divorced are no longer legally bound to their spouse. The word divorced describes a certain person's state in life, just like the married describes a person's state. A person moves from the category "married" to the category "divorced."

Divorce may only be thought of as negative, but divorce is often healthy and positive. To divorce means to detach oneself from some sort of wrong or evil. One might say, "I need to divorce myself from that hurtful way of thinking." When one has taken the steps to separate oneself from dishonorable people or events, one properly says, "I took action and divorced myself from the horrible situation."

A DIVORCE STATISTIC

A "statistic" is a fact or piece of data from a study of a large quantity of numerical data. A statistic is an event or a person regarded as a piece of data. Being divorced means an individual is a divorce statistic. I was hypersensitive and inappropriately placed a particular category above life itself. Like the word divorce, I only saw being a statistic as a negative. I was afraid of becoming a divorce statistic, that kept me in an unhealthy marriage.

Being a "marriage statistic," while likely not thought of that way by the persons getting married, is honorable. Marriage is generally a public event, intentionally shared in community for the purpose of celebration. Divorce is private, painfully private. The isolation of divorce may leave the broken individuals feeling like an impersonal, cold hard fact to be studied. Being a divorce statistic is not honorable, in fact it is often even viewed as shameful. The church cries out, "There are too many divorce statistics! We have to protect the institution of marriage."

The fear of being "that divorce statistic" kept me silent. Church leaders told me, "we have to save your marriage." "You have to learn to communicate better, you have to try harder" was their demand. The sinking feeling was so heavy it was nearly unbearable. My breath was shallow and tight in my chest. After much discernment and prayer, I separated from my spouse. After a time, I initiated the process of divorce and was well on my way to becoming divorced and a divorce statistic. Thirty years earlier I had boldly and innocently stated, "I will never get divorced." I had failed my own expectations and the church's standard and bigger yet, I believed I had failed God.

The breakdown of a marriage and a home is a tumultuous time, that likely includes at least some degree of emotional breakdown. Emotional breakdown often leads to individuals becoming other sorts of statistics. Honesty about the reality some have lived is critical. Many live in fear for their lives. There is the very real possibility in cases of domestic violence for murder or murder/suicide to take place. There is also the very real possibility for a person in crisis to commit suicide. Another form of spiritual death, a very slow death, is depression. Depression feels like a place of no hope, a place of despair.

Despair breeds loneliness, isolation and hopelessness. Hope and healing shatter loneliness and despair. In order for individuals to make their way through crisis, the focus must be on the human being, not the divorce they have been through or the statistic they are.

HUMAN BEINGS

In the midst of the crisis and despair, one of the greatest challenges is for people to embrace their value as human beings. We cannot simply pay lip service to this critical fact, we must dive in deeply to embrace people as living, valuable, breathing human beings. Feeling valueless abounds in a culture where the institution of the church or marriage is viewed as of higher value than an individual person. We must journey forward, clinging to the fact that being divorced may describe one's state in life, but it does not define a person's being or heart. Being married did not or at least should not define an individual; being divorced does not or should not define an individual.

What does it mean to be a living, breathing human being? This question sounds trite, but the answer is of utmost importance. A significant part of the complex answer is found in our God's creative touch and breath. The Scriptures say, "Then the Lord God formed man of dust from the ground, and breathed into his nostrils the breath of life; and man became a living being," (Genesis 2:7, NASB) The second half of the verse was formative for me, especially after I studied the very significant

Hebrew words translated *living* and *being*. "Living" is the word *chay*, meaning to make alive the whole person. The word translated "being" is the Hebrew word *nephesh*, that encompasses the whole of life, breath, heart, soul, and spirit. *Nephesh* indicates the entire person, including the inner self. The author of this verse used these two words to underscore God's creative work. God created a whole, living human being, by his very breath, to live life fully alive.

Breath and a beating heart keep the human body alive, but is one truly living in every sense of the word as God designed? In my particular circumstance, crisis brought shallowness of breath, a tightening of my emotions, and a slow shutting down of my soul and spirit. My world had narrowed to an unhealthy definition of me and marriage. My marriage defined my being and affected every aspect of life. I couldn't breathe.

The breath of God saved me. I slowly gave up the notion that I could personally defend the institution of marriage with my life. I began caring for my internal being, and I learned to be kind and loving to myself. Silence, shame and depression lost their hold on me as I clung to the breath of God in me. I visualized my life coming alive and being healed, as Peter says, "in Christ's wounds," (1Peter 2:24). I slowly learned (and continue to learn) to grasp hold of God's full acceptance just simply because I am alive. These concepts should have been deeply engraved in my being, but they were so very difficult to grasp, "for me" in the midst of crisis.

Another aspect of being a living, breathing human being is living in community. We cannot reside in the very empty space of isolation and truly live. I tried to live there until illness and pain led me to medical professionals. They became very concerned about both my physical and emotional health. Their questions cut deep into my soul: "Do you know you are barely breathing?" "What is causing your fear?" My instinct was to reply, "I am breathing" and "I am not afraid." But I had a choice. I could continue ignoring my health, or I could pay closer attention to my being and ask for help.

Asking for help, I have learned, is an act of courage! I repeat, focusing on one's life and reaching out for help from proper channels is courageous. Many falsely believe that self-care is selfish. Tragically, many church leaders preach "it is better to give than to receive," completely missing one of the main themes of Scripture: "receiving is one of the highest forms of giving." Receiving allows us to rest, a treasure that often eludes those in crisis. Receiving gives us strength and wisdom to grow as well as to give. Medical professionals, therapists, counselors, and ministers with experience in trauma counseling are human beings God works through to help people make sense of the confusing world in which they live.

Addressing self-care, a care for the whole being—heart, soul, mind, body, and spirit—can be a daunting task. The process of the journey into healing is just that, a slow process of growth into a deeper understanding of God's magnificent love and care for human beings. Believing that one is valuable as a breathing, living human being ushers in hope in the midst of despair, deep pain, and trauma.

We are valuable simply because we are alive and breathing. We need to define ourselves by God's definition of us, hope-filled and freed, redeemed by Christ. We need hope in the midst of the trauma of a marriage coming to an end and the recovery associated with being divorced. We need redemption and creative life, the breath of life in us. We are being called to grow up in Christ, called to learn deep within our hearts and souls that our value to our Creator was and is simply because God created us. Our value as a human being is not found in our accomplishments, including our ability to stay married or to not be a divorce statistic.

LIFE IN MY VINEYARD

My family vineyard on California's Central Coast provided a profound place in which to learn to breathe and grow. Each and every day I focused on the deep roots of the vine in the soil of the land that has been our family's home for many generations. I focused on the sap that flows at all times in the vine, even though I could not see the energy working. As I drove tractor, I watched in awe as the tender shoots reached for the sunlight in the spring and then dipped down in summer and fall with the weight of the fruit.

Christ's words, I am the Vine; you are the branches, abide in me (see John 15:4-5) became more and more meaningful as I focused on an activity I had been privileged to witness in my vineyard—grafting. Grafting is the process of inserting a twig or bud into a rooted, non-fruit bearing vine. Grafting can be likened to the medical procedure of transplanting a piece of skin on a wound. Here are some of my observations. (*The Vine Speaks,* Concordia Publishing House, 2013.)

Rootstock is a hardy home for a varietal such as Cabernet Sauvignon. We graft onto rootstock because it is disease resistant and we can choose a specific rootstock to match our Paso Robles, CA heat and drought. Grafting takes place one time in the life of a vine, most often in a nursery prior to the vines being delivered to the vineyard. One year, grafting took place in our field, giving me opportunity to witness the action. I watched closely as teams of three workers grafted the vines.

Team member one cut a "v" shaped slice into the flesh of a rootstock that had been growing in our field for one year. Team member two had branches of Cabernet Sauvignon in a pouch hanging from his side. He took one branch at a time in hand and cut tiny "v" shaped buds from the branch. I looked closely and saw a bud at each leaf on the branch. Each bud contains all of the fruit and shoot growth for the following year. Team member two placed the tiny bud of Cabernet Sauvignon into the perfectly shaped slice in the flesh of the root stock.

Team member three wrapped a Band-Aid® like substance around the wound. I learned that the sap flows so rapidly to the wound to begin the healing process that a bandage needs to hold the bud in place until the wound heals. With this grafting process, the rootstock becomes the home for the varietal for the entire 30 to 50-year life of the vine.

The image became profoundly clear—Christ, the vine, is resistant to disease and death; I am the bud, the branch of the vine, grafted into His life. Christ is my home; Christ, the Root, is my stability. My forever home, my abiding space "in" the very life of Christ is secure. The Band-Aid® symbolizes healing in the wounds of Christ. The Apostle Peter declared, "by his wounds we are healed," (1 Peter 2:24). I cherished the image of my "home" in Christ. I also compared my home in Christ with my tumultuous earthly home.

My earthly home was not at that time a place of safety or rest. As I meditated in the health of the Root, Christ Jesus, I slowly took on the courage to break the silence and shame, admitting that our dating, engagement and marriage had been violated with anger and violence. The sap flow provided a rich image of the life I lived "in" Christ, having been grafted into his life by God, the Master Gardener. The growth of the vines in my vineyard provided an intense call to grow up in the knowledge of Christ's breath in me, urging me to live. The changing seasons in the vineyard provided a vivid picture of hope.

I held to the hope that in spite of having learned and lived to date with an unhealthy internal world, I could learn a healthy way of living life as a human being, alive, and breathing. My very being was broken and in deep pain; my cry was real and raw. I didn't want to be a divorce statistic, but I knew living was God's call for me. The vine, the roots, the sap and the seasons guided my journey. Embracing Christ's words in the Scriptures "for me" led me deeply into the stories of Jesus' words and work in the lives of broken people. One particular story in Christ's journey took on real significance for me.

A STATISTIC STORY; A REDEMPTION STORY

There was a dusty road in Samaria, a path unfamiliar to Jesus' disciples and avoided by religious leaders. At the ancient well of Jacob, Jesus engaged in a conversation with a woman. Jesus declared Himself living water. Jesus proclaimed Himself the long-awaited Messiah to a broken-hearted woman whose statistics are an important part of the story.

Jesus knew the woman's statistics. "Jesus said to her, 'Go, call your husband, and come here.' The woman answered Him, 'I have no husband.' Jesus said to her, 'You are right in saying, I have no husband; for you have had five husbands, and the one you now have is not your husband. What you have said is true'" (John 4:16-18). In Jesus' eyes and heart, this woman was a human being, valuable simply because she was alive. Rather than fade away into shame at the statistics, the woman trusted Jesus, that led to a profound discussion of worship, and to the woman and her community worshipping Christ.

Jesus loved her as an alive human being. He knew her fully, better than she knew herself. He stated the truth of her statistics. Amazingly, it was her very own story, her statistics, that became her most powerful witness to her community! "When she returned to her village many in her town believed in Jesus because of her testimony, 'Come, see a man who told me all that I ever did. Can this be the Christ?'" (John 4:29).

The statistic five husbands and living with one who was not her husband leaves many open-ended questions. We don't know her whole story. John, Jesus' disciple, focused on Jesus' redemption of her life, rather than why she had these statistics. Rather than leave it in the unknown category and focus on Jesus' redemptive word and work in her heart, soul, spirit, and mind, many feel the need to pontificate about her as an outcast. This begs the question, "Why would anyone listen to her if she had been rejected by her community?"

"He told me all that I ever did" was her launch point of witnessing her faith in the Messiah. She was not silenced in shame by Jesus, she was excited that He knew her fully and redeemed her, redeemed her entire life story. Her powerful testimony led many to invite Jesus to stay in their community, "So when the Samaritans came to him, they asked Him to stay with them, and He stayed there two days. And many more believed because of His word. They said to the woman, 'It is no longer because of what you said that we believe, for we have heard for ourselves, and we know that this is indeed the Savior of the world'" (John 4:40-42).

Jesus' word and work, His life as living water, flowed freely from Himself into the lives of the people in this story, in the context of their very real human stories. The woman worshiped Jesus by receiving His life, His word, His work for her. She did not attempt to offer her stories or her life as a sacrifice, she received Jesus at His word as the final sacrifice, the Messiah, the descendant of "her father Jacob." This is a profoundly important lesson for us—we are called to receive and rejoice in Christ's words in our story, not apart from our stories.

This well-educated woman with less than desirable statistics, and Jesus, the long-awaited one, had a profoundly personal conversation that ended with these words, "I know that Messiah is coming (he who is called Christ). When he comes, he will tell us all things." Jesus said to her, "I who speak to you am He" (John 4:25 -26). She and her community had been waiting in expectant faith and hope for this very conversation!

We have waited and the time is now here for heart to heart conversation with Christ and with one another. We are human beings, each with our own statistics, our unique stories, loved by Christ Jesus with a love so powerful it swallows our statistics and silences our condemning self-doubt. Jesus knows our statistics; He knows our stories; He redeems us in our stories. He calls us to rise up out of silence and shame in order to testify along with the woman at the well, "He told me everything I've ever done."

CHAPTER 2

God Hates Divorce—What? And Why?

"I hate divorce" (Malachi 2:16 NASB) are God's words through the Prophet Malachi, written 450 years before the birth of Christ. These three words are often quoted by church leaders in sermons or counseling. "God hates divorce" flows from the mouths of individuals who believe they are protecting the institution of marriage or that they can save marriages. The context of the words, "I hate divorce" is of utmost importance as we seek to more fully understand life in our stories of divorce.

People were discouraged and the crops had been bad. They had expected to prosper with God as their God, after their return from Babylonian captivity. The people questioned God's love asking, "How have you loved us?" (Malachi 1:2). Careless priests were misusing the temple, misusing sacrifices to God and misleading a confused people. The priests challenged God's word through Malachi asking, "How have we defiled you?" (Malachi 1:7).

The name of God was being defiled. The leadership was in chaos and the people were being misled in the midst of that chaos. God could not tolerate the misuse of His name and declared, "For from the rising of the sun to its setting my name will be great among the nations, and in every place, incense will be offered to my name, and a pure offering. For my name will be great among the nations, says the Lord of hosts," (Malachi 1:11).

God promised a messenger who would clear the way, one who would be like a refiner's fire. His judgment would be sharp and clean. No one would be able to stand in the presence of His judgment! The prophet Malachi also declared these words of comfort, "But for you who fear my name, the sun of righteousness shall rise with healing in its wings. You shall go out leaping like calves from the stall. And you shall tread down the wicked, for they will be ashes under the soles of your feet, on the day when I act, says the Lord of hosts," (Malachi 4:2-3).

There is no mistaking the word of God. Those who defile God's name and misuse His mercy will pay the price of God's judgment. Those who trust God's word will be healed and raised up. As with all of God's word in the Old Testament, the word pointed to the Christ, the one who would come to bear the weight of all sin, receive God's judgment, pay the price with His very life and be raised up from the grave by a holy God. Christ's ransom (lutron) would be God's pure gift for all who trust Him.

PROBLEM ONE—THEN

The book of Malachi is, in large part, a rebuke of religious leaders. God had placed priests to lead, but instead they were misleading the people by their words and actions. Waiting for the promised Messiah faithfully was God's call to the leaders, a call that included speaking the word of God clearly and leading a life as an example of God's mercy. "For the lips of a priest should guard knowledge, and people should seek instruction from his mouth, for he is the messenger of the Lord of hosts," (Malachi 2:7).

Malachi rebukes the leaders saying "you are dealing treacherously and faithlessly" with one another. Malachi's rebuke follows God's clear intent for His word and covenant, "But you have turned aside from the way. You have caused many to stumble by your instruction. You have corrupted the covenant of Levi," (Malachi 2:8). Malachi's questions take God's harsh rebuke a step further, "Have we not all one Father? Has not one God created us? Why then are we faithless to one another, profaning the covenant of our fathers?" (Malachi 2:10).

Religious leaders were rebuked and chastised for causing people to stumble by using their stature as a platform to misuse the word of God. Their unfaithfulness to God, as well as to the brides of their youth, caused great harm to the hearts of the people they were called to lead. Rather than take stock of their own spirits and humble their hearts and lives before God, they were stubborn in spirit.

> And this second thing you do. You cover the Lord's altar with tears, with weeping and groaning because he no longer regards the offering or accepts it with favor from your hand. But you say, "Why does he not?" Because the Lord was witness between you and the wife of your youth, to whom you have been faithless, though she is your companion and your wife by covenant. Did he not make them one, with a portion of the Spirit in their union? And what was the one God seeking? Godly offspring. So guard yourselves in your spirit, and let none of you be faithless to the wife of your youth. "For the man who does not love his wife but divorces her, says the Lord, the God of Israel, covers his garment with violence, says the Lord of hosts. So guard yourselves in your spirit, and do not be faithless," (Malachi 2:13-16).

The English Standard Version (ESV) translation of verses 15 and 16 place God's anger squarely on the priest, the religious leader who was faithless to his bride. God was a witness to their union and blessed their oneness with His Spirit. God's burning question through Malachi was "Did He not make them one with a portion of the Spirit?" God called the priests to "guard yourselves in your spirit" that would lead to a healthy desire for relationship with God and with the wife of his youth. Lack of guarding the spirit led to faithlessness to both God and the priest's bride. Faithlessness led to violence.

The verses above quoted from the ESV have not created the historical misuse of the words "I hate divorce" and "God hates divorce." The New American Standard Bible (NASB, 1971, 1995) translation of verses 15 and 16 follows here so we can understand the historical problem, as well as the harm that can be done when taking these words out of context: "Take heed then to your spirit, and let no one deal treacherously against the wife of your youth. 'For I hate divorce,' says the Lord, the God of Israel, 'and him who covers his garment with wrong,' says the Lord of hosts. 'So take heed to your spirit, that you do not deal treacherously.'" Malachi 2:15b-16 (NASB)

"For I hate divorce" has historically been pulled out of the middle of a chapter, out of the middle of a sentence in one chapter of the whole Bible. "I hate divorce" is quoted apart from context as well as apart from the words treacherous and wrong. The sentence reads, "For I hate divorce and him who covers his garment with wrong." God speaks His hatred into the wrong done by religious leaders who were tasked with speaking His word faithfully. God's words called priests to pay attention to their spirits so they would not deal treacherously with their wives.

Treacherous means faithless, with deception or betrayal. To deal treacherously with someone to whom you have made a promise before God is offensive to God. In this instance religious leaders were betraying God by betraying their wives. They betrayed God by dealing treacherously with their wives in their own homes. By doing so, they were misleading the people they were called to lead. God hates this divorce and this wrong.

The words violence (ESV) and wrong (NASB) are the Hebrew word *châmâc* meaning "to hurt, tear down, oppress, do deal with wickedly." Malachi's words from God were directed at religious leaders who were mistreating their wives and misusing their marriages while claiming to speak the word of God. "I hate divorce" was spoken as a rebuke to unruly priests who were not valuing and cherishing the wife of their youth. They were dealing treacherously and with violence in the marriage relationship to which God had been a witness. Priests were to be examples of God's love, starting in their own homes, and from there to the people. Malachi said, "You have wearied the Lord with your words," (Malachi 2:17a).

These words were a wakeup call to religious leaders who dealt treacherously and violently with their wives. They also misused God's words that created further violence in the lives of men and women who were being forced to live in treachery and wrong in their homes. God spoke, "I hate divorce and him who covers his garment with wrong" directly into the evil being done in the homes of priests. Is misuse of Scripture today any different than the misuse of the word of God in the days of the prophet Malachi?

PROBLEM TWO—NOW

"I hate divorce" was preached from the pulpit when I was teenager. This preacher, I later learned, committed great wrong in his own home against his wife and daughter. Misuse flourishes because the phrase "I hate divorce" is pulled out of context and preached to those hungry for the true word of God. Religious leaders speaking "I hate divorce" without discussing what it means to deal in violence and treachery against a spouse is both wrong and dangerous. Quoting "I hate divorce" from the pulpit apart from a discussion of what it means for a man to guard his spirit and cherish the wife of his youth is tragic. Religious leaders preaching "God hates divorce" apart from living out the word of God in their homes is a slap in the face of our God, who desires truth and mercy.

I recall only quick, uncomfortable words spoken about divorce. Sadly, the feeling of disgust comes to my heart as I recall others discussing the divorces of our friends as they gossiped about their lives. Innocently or not, I remember hearing adults confidently say, "Marriage is 50/50, both make it work and if it doesn't work both are equally at fault." Unspoken words screamed louder yet. There was no teaching about misuse or abuse of a living, breathing human being. There was utter silence about broken hearts or healing. Healthy marriage, sexuality, and sex were not discussed either.

My heart breaks when I recall my life experiences with religious leaders misusing the word of God and abusing human life. I have learned as an adult that during my childhood there were three different religious leaders who were sexually abusive to either their spouses or children. I spoke of one of the men above, another preacher had an affair with the church secretary. During my years in youth ministry I served with a minister who was arrested for sexually abusing his grandchild. He was convicted of sexual assault and as part of his sentencing admitted abusing many of the young people in the congregation. He served a life sentence and eventually died in prison.

The experiences of my youth with abuse, without knowing what it was, as well as with watching divorce taking place around me, framed my internal understanding of marriage. It was assumed that I would get married. It was an unspoken rule that I would remain sexually pure for marriage. It was taken for granted that I would be happy and stay married. My mantra became, "I will never get a divorce."

My internal understanding of life was guided by these two categories, "I am a sinner" and "God forgives me because Jesus died on the cross to save me from my sins." While true statements, much was left to discern in my young mind in the context of a culture where challenging topics like sexuality, sex, marriage, and divorce were avoided in the hopes that I would figure it out or that my questions would simply go away. I had not developed the important skill set to recognize or deal with someone's sins against me. I married young and brought with me the brokenness of unhealthy church life, as well as the pain and shame from sexual assault in a previous dating relationship.

From the above context, I did my best with the challenges of violent anger in my home by apologizing and promising to be better. I innocently and dangerously believed that if I just loved someone more, they would be kind and loving back to me. An immature faith, a broken heart and an insecure mind led me to improperly deduce, "God hates divorce, if I divorce God will hate me." Those deeply ingrained thoughts were not conscious, but they were present as was deep pain and fear of failure.

THE TRUTH

Misuse of a true statement does not make God's word or demand untrue. God's statement through Malachi "for I hate divorce" flowed from God's heart. Unfaithfulness to God and to one another cannot breed life. God called religious leaders to turn their minds and hearts from their evil ways, to turn toward Him, away from violence and treachery. God called the priests and all people to cherish the gift of life and love the spouse of their youth.

Voicing truth into the darkness of the abuse of the word of God flows from the hearts of those freed by the truth. The truth is, God hates divorce. We must come to grips with the fact that God hates all things that would come between God and His people. God's holy hatred includes hating the hard-hearted leaders who silence people by false use of His word. Voicing truth into darkness means speaking light into darkness and speaking Christ into darkness.

God's holy hatred toward anything that separates us from Him was taken out in the perfect ransom (lutron) of the life of His Son. Christ, the perfect sacrifice through His sinless life, suffering, and death was the one and only ransom accepted by a holy God. God's mercy in Christ swallows up our fear of God's wrath and hatred. Trusting in Christ's mercy for us breeds hope and hope breeds courage to live life. Trusting in Christ's mercy gives us courage to call for the proper use of God's word. Proper use of the word of God leads people to a deeper faith in Christ's word and work on their behalf as the ransom through His very life.

God ordained marriage and marriage is His gift. The covenant relationship between one man and one woman for life is given by God, designed by God to be a mirror of God's covenant relationship to His people. God's institution of marriage and the covenant of marriage does not outweigh the lives of the people in the marriage. Guarding an institution cannot trump guarding the hearts and lives of the individuals in the marriage.

Health, growth, cherishing, and sacrificial love are to be exhibited in marriage; forgiveness and mercy are to be central to the bond between husband and wife. In that covenant God seeks Godly offspring in order to continue His lineage (Malachi 2:15). Godly offspring are born both when children are brought into this world as well as when "children" of faith are nurtured through the love exhibited in the marriage. The life-breeding covenant of marriage, the one-flesh union between man and woman, is intended by the Creator of marriage to bring life, breath and health in all possible ways.

Abuse of the gift of God takes place when lives are dying, breath is being stripped away under the violence and control of those who would deal treacherously. "I hate divorce" is often used by religious leaders against men and women who are being sinned against. Bondage upon bondage is bred by using of the holy word of God against people who are often in grave danger for their very lives. This is wrong and this is evil.

Redemption through divorce takes place through the very life of Christ. Redeemed, freed, people made holy by the blood of Christ rejoice in God's mercy and love for them. Malachi's words from God, "I hate divorce," understood in the proper context, give us much to ponder about honoring the marriage covenant between God and His people as well as the God-ordained covenant between husbands and wives. This leads us to other portions of Old Testament Scripture where God works through divorce to call a faithless people to redemption.

CHAPTER 3

God's Divorce—What? And Why?

God is divorced. God, creator, sinless, and almighty, is a divorce statistic. This shocking fact leads to important questions: Why? What were Israel and Judah's offenses leading God to issue a certificate of divorce? Why did He send them away? What can we learn from God's work through the very thing He hates? How can we understand God's divorce as an act of redemption? How can the words of the prophets Jeremiah and Ezekiel call us into a deeper relationship with God from the context of our divorce or the broken lives of someone we love?

God is just and His divorce is completely justified. We cannot compare ourselves or justify ourselves in His presence in any life state, whether married, divorced, or single. He is creator, we are creatures; He is holy, we must be covered by Christ's righteous sacrifice in order to stand before a holy God. These premises will provide the structure for our study of the Old Testament word of God through the prophets who proclaimed Judah and Israel unfaithful and sent them away with a certificate of divorce.

OLD TESTAMENT IMAGERY—
JEREMIAH 2 & 3, EZEKIEL 16

The prophets Jeremiah and Ezekiel were charged with the daunting task of speaking the word of God to a stubborn, hard-hearted people. They told them, repent and turn away from your evil ways on behalf of a patient God who had chosen a covenant relationship with Israel and Judah. He had set them apart to be His own. He married them and was jealous for their love and full dedication to Him in their marriage.

Israel and Judah, formerly a beautiful bride, were no longer dedicated to their marriage to God. God directed Jeremiah, "Go and proclaim in the hearing of Jerusalem, thus says the Lord, 'I remember the devotion of your youth, your love as a bride, how you followed me in the wilderness, in a land not sown. What wrong did your fathers find in me that they went far from me, and went after worthlessness and became worthless'" (Jeremiah 2:2 & 5)? Ezekiel told the story of God's covenant with His bride, "When I passed by you again and saw you, behold, you were at the age for love, and I spread the corner of my garment over you and covered your nakedness; I made my vow to you and entered into a covenant with you, declares the Lord God, and you became mine" (Ezekiel 16:8).

Sadly, here are the actions of God's beautiful bride, "You trusted in your beauty and played the whore because of your renown and lavished your whorings on any passerby; your beauty became his. You took some of your garments and made for yourself colorful shrines, and on them played the whore. The like has never been, nor ever shall be. You also took your beautiful jewels of my gold and of my silver, which I had given you, and made for yourself images of men, and with them played the whore" (Ezekiel 16:15-17).

The word "whore" is a very strong word meaning a prostitute or one who sells him or herself. Adultery, another strong word, is also used in the Scriptures to describe the offenses Israel and Judah committed against God. The following list of whorings and adulteries is taken from Jeremiah chapters 2 & 3 and Ezekiel chapter 16:

- Ate the first fruits that were to be set aside as an offering to God
- Defiled land and made God's heritage an abomination
- Prophesied by Baal rather than only on behalf of God
- Devoured the prophets of God with swords
- Went after things that do not profit
- Changed gods
- Forsook God
- Bowed down like a whore on every high hill and under every green tree
- Forgot God

- Said, "I have not sinned"
- Sat awaiting lovers
- Did all the evil they could
- Polluted the land committing adultery, Jeremiah states, "with stone and tree"
- Returned to God with pretense
- Trusted in their beauty and played the whore
- Lavished their whorings on any passerby
- Took their beautiful jewels of God's gold and God's silver, that he had given them, and made images of men, and played the whore with them
- Sacrificed their sons and daughters to be devoured

The long list of adulteries committed by Israel and Judah shatter the notion that committing adultery can be narrowed to sexual events by married individuals outside the covenant of marriage. We can summarize adultery in modern terminology with these words, affairs, addiction, and abuse. Adultery in the form of affairs, addiction, and abuse cover a vast array of ways in which the marriage covenant is violated. These violations bring great confusion and harm upon hearts created by God to experience life through healthy relationships.

God's rich love for His bride persisted even though she had committed many adulteries. In spite of His hatred of divorce, God sent Israel away with a certificate of divorce. Jeremiah recorded, "She [Judah] saw that for all the adulteries of that faithless one, Israel, I had sent her away with a decree of divorce. Yet her treacherous sister Judah did not fear, but she too went and played the whore" (Jeremiah 3:8).

God's divorce was purposeful and He worked through divorce for the purpose of redemption. Divorce served as a means through which He called His people away from their adulteries, back to Himself. Ezekiel's words point to Christ's sacrifice for His bride: "'I will establish my covenant with you, and you shall know that I am the Lord, that you may remember and be confounded, and never open your mouth again because of your shame, when I atone for you for all that you have done,' declares the Lord God" (Ezekiel 16:62-63).

God wanted the bride of His youth back and He could take her back only by atonement. This seems contrary to the very law God had established! God asked a pointed question, "If a man divorces his wife and she goes from him and becomes another man's wife, will he return to her? Would not that land be greatly polluted? You have played the whore with many lovers; and would you return to Me?' declares the Lord" (Jeremiah 3:1). God would take His bride back only on His terms—redemption, atonement that would be spoken from the mouth of Christ and accomplished by the True Shepherd, Christ Jesus.

> Go, and proclaim these words toward the north, and say, Return, faithless Israel, declares the Lord. I will not look on you in anger, for I am merciful, declares the Lord; I will not be angry forever. Only acknowledge your guilt, that you rebelled against the Lord your God and scattered

> your favors among foreigners under every green tree, and that you have not obeyed my voice, declares the Lord. Return, O faithless children, declares the Lord; for I am your master; I will take you, one from a city and two from a family, and I will bring you to Zion. And I will give you shepherds after my own heart, who will feed you with knowledge and understanding.'" Jeremiah 3:12-15

Jeremiah's call to the sons of Israel was the call of redemption, to return and be healed. The people's response to that call was the cry, "everything we have followed was a delusion, truly in the Lord our God is the salvation of Israel." Jeremiah said,

> And they shall no more stubbornly follow their own evil heart. Surely, as a treacherous wife leaves her husband, so have you been treacherous to me, O house of Israel," declares the Lord. A voice on the bare heights is heard, the weeping and pleading of Israel's sons because they have perverted their way; they have forgotten the Lord their God. "Return, O faithless sons; I will heal your faithlessness." "Behold, we come to you, for you are the Lord our God. Truly the hills are a delusion, the orgies on the mountains. Truly in the Lord our God is the salvation of Israel." Jeremiah 3:17, 20-23

The words of Jeremiah and Ezekiel point to the Christ and declare that only through Christ could an unfaithful, divorced bride return to God. Israel and Judah repented and turned from their adulterous ways; God received them back. Only God could accomplish the atonement, the release of captives from captivity through redemption. In Christ's perfect life, death and resurrection the Bridegroom redeems His bride for a holy purpose. Zechariah, holding the infant Jesus, proclaimed, "Blessed be the Lord God of Israel, for He has visited and redeemed (lutrōsis) His people and has raised up a horn of salvation for us in the house of His servant David, as He spoke by the mouth of His holy prophets from of old" (Luke 1:68-69).

REDEMPTION THROUGH DIVORCE

God worked redemption through divorce. He worked redemption through divorcing Israel and He works redemption through divorce today. God continues to pursue the people He loves, working through all circumstances. Wake up to my perfect love for you is God's fervent call as He continues to work through all things to call us to Himself. He is jealous for our love and faithfulness; He pursues us where we are, here and now, so He can lavish His love on us.

Christ pursues us and in His infinite love works in many ways to draw us to Himself. Hopefully, through the call of the word of God, individuals repent, turn, and receive Christ's redemption. If turning and receiving does not take place, God works in another important way. Those wounded by a vast array of adulteries serve as agents of Christ's work by speaking a courageous "no" to the adultery. God also works by hardening stubborn hearts even further through the voice of the one suffering from the offense or by the voice of the advocates of that individual. There are circumstances where one's voice speaks a loud call to redemption by demanding divorce.

God has always worked through divorce and will continue to do so. Restoration of the marriage may or may not be possible. God is at work, both in redemption through marriage and redemption through divorce. God pursues us with His perfect love just as He passionately pursued Israel and Judah. Christ's perfect love and His work of redemption will guide our journey as we continue to understand ourselves as human beings, created by God for relationship with Him and for healthy relationships with one another.

CHAPTER 4

Hope

What is hope? What do we place our hope in? Hope is defined as a feeling of expectation and a desire for a certain thing to happen. We may hope our team wins or hope for a better crop. We may hope our surgery goes well or that our friend doesn't die. We may place our hope in the stock market or solid interest rates. Certain types of expectations or hopes are within our control, such as I hope for a better crop, therefore I will take steps to farm my vineyard with these practices. Other circumstances are beyond our control. We must rely on a doctor or on medical teams when we are seriously ill.

Hope takes a different tone when we ask, "In whom do we place our hope?" When the feeling of expectation and a desire for a certain thing to happen relies on God, faith and trust must be present. When our hopes in a particular person for a lifelong marriage were dashed, we had every opportunity to be disappointed in or even blame God. As we know, God hears our frustration and anger, but blaming God doesn't get us moving toward healing. We humbly confess that God's design for marriage is not flawed. Hope is something bigger than a person or an institution. We proceed by exploring Christ as the one in whom we place our hope, trust, and faith.

Christ, alone, is the One in whom we place our hope. He is redeemer who redeems (apoluō) in all circumstances including our individual stories of divorce. Christ alone is light and life, the perfect One who lived and died in our place. Christ is the redeemer, our redemption (lutrōsis) sets free and liberates (apoluō) a people in bondage by the ransom (lutron) of His very life. Christ's ransom sets us free. Christ, the promised one, had been the object of hope, of expectant waiting as the deliverer of freedom.

Two people, as we've highlighted, were gifted with witnessing their expectant hope met in the baby Jesus' entrance into this world. Zechariah cried out, "Blessed be the Lord God of Israel, for He has visited and redeemed (lutrōsis) His people," (Luke 1:68). Anna, the prophetess, gave thanks to God and spoke of the Christ to all who were waiting for redemption (Luke 2:37b-38, paraphrased).

We wait too, in redemption hope, longing to be visited by Christ. We want to know Him intimately, to experience life. God created us and all people with this God-breathed desire to know Him and hope in Him. We were created for a life of hope and with an internal longing for His love and for deep connection with Him.

Hope became more alive for me as I meditated on my position of abiding and resting, grafted into Christ's life. I also meditated on Christ' life alive in me. Jesus said, "Abide in me and I in you," (John 15:4a). The visual of Christ as my root and myself grafted into His life became a powerful force of hope in my heart and mind. Growing in faith and love led me to grasp hold of truth that Christ is my dwelling place, my home. I pictured the roots of the vines in my vineyard growing to a depth of ten to fifteen feet into the harsh soil. I mediated on the Scripture verses that point to Christ as the eternal root. I pictured my life *in* His life and my life *in* the stories as He walked this earth.

Hope guided my growth into a deeper understanding that Christ dwells in my heart through faith. This sounds elementary, but paying attention to Christ in my heart had not been part of my internal world. I was much more comfortable with head knowledge. Education and knowledge are wonderful gifts; however, those two best friends had become my place to hide from life. We likely know about Christ as redeemer from years in the faith and good education; that is good, but it is head knowledge. We were created with a hunger to know Him intimately in our heart. We long for the love of God in Christ for us, in our hearts, for us. In the midst of despair, the flicker of hope helped me keep my eyes fixed on me in Christ and Christ in me.

Fear of not knowing myself and the lack of skills to "think about how I think" almost paralyzed me in despair and depression. Courage and the desire to deeply know Christ's love and to live life in the freedom Christ won "for me" gave me hope and proved to be more powerful than my fear. I embarked on my journey as a married woman, fully committed to stay married for life. For years I worked with all my might on me and vowed to bring my spouse along in the journey of hope, into Christ's love and mercy.

The Scriptures were my daily friend and companion. I dove into Christ's story from the context of my story. I'd read and pray early, then go fulfill my tasks in the vineyard—tractor driving, irrigation or harvest. I meditated on the word of God throughout my busy days farming the vines with my father. Redemption hope, for me, led me on a journey of trusting Christ at His word and work for me.

QUESTIONS

An amazing exercise developed as I journeyed in hope. I wrote out every question Jesus asked during His time on earth and I meditated on those questions, in the context of the stories. I also wrote down every question people asked Jesus. Journaling the questions recorded in the Gospels was powerful and revealed important categories. Some followed Jesus wholeheartedly, some followed and eventually left, others turned their hearts against Him.

The profound questions Jesus asked of those who placed their hope in Him ushered in a deeper relationship of the heart with Him. His questions were hope-filled and a call away from self-reliance. Hope, faith, trust, and love was Christ's call. He received and answered the questions of those who followed Him. Their desire for a deeper relationship with the One True God brought many challenges as they journeyed with Jesus, but hope in Him and an intimate relationship with Him kept many people by His side.

Those who followed Jesus for a time must have watched carefully as Christ worked on this earth. They watched Jesus heal the sick, make the blind see and the deaf hear. They were fed by Jesus' word as well as His miracle of turning a few loaves of bread and a couple fish into enough food for thousands. Eventually, many turned away because they determined that following Jesus was too hard.

Many of Jesus' questions were directed to those with hard hearts. His questions trapped religious leaders in their harsh theological premises, false piety, and hypocrisy. These leaders made exhaustive attempts to trap Jesus with their questions. Jesus knew their hearts and answered many of their questions with questions. His tactic masterfully revealed their hard hearts and the hardness of their hearts escalated to an even greater degree. Scriptures reveal a time in which religious leaders simply stopped asking Jesus questions (see Mark 12). Religious leaders lived devout lives in their head, apart from expectant hope and merciful love flowing from their hearts. Their knowledge protected them, so they thought, but it was their knowledge that hardened them to Christ's word and work.

Questions Jesus asked of two different people played an important role in my journey from despair into hope. "What do you want me to do for you?" (Matthew 20:32, Mark 10:36, 51, Luke 18:41)? And "Do you want to be healed" (John 5:6)? These were questions Jesus asked of humble, hurting people. I took the courage to allow Jesus to ask me those same questions, hopeful that He was there for me. One of the scariest aspects of the journey was wrestling with the fact that the answers to those two challenging questions weren't immediately available. I call these types of questions journey questions. For me, these frightening questions were also hope-filled questions that guided me to deeper trust in Christ.

I pondered the questions of the religious leaders as well. Their questions can be summarized by these two questions: "Jesus, how much can we get away with and still follow the law of Moses?" And, "Jesus, how much can we get away with and still follow you?" Both questions had roots in one stubborn, arrogant demand: Jesus must follow them or suffer the consequences of blasphemy against their god.

QUESTIONS ABOUT DIVORCE

One of the religious leader's questions designed to test Jesus was, "Is it lawful to divorce one's wife for any cause?" (Matthew 19:3)? Jesus' answer set forth the beauty of God's design for one man and one woman to be in a loving, kind, one-flesh relationship. They continued to question Jesus, asking "Why then did Moses command one to give a certificate of divorce and to send her away?" (Matthew 19:7). He said to them, "Because of your hardness of heart Moses allowed you to divorce your wives, but from the beginning it was not so," (Matthew 19:8).

Moses' decree allowed a certificate of divorce to be issued by a man to release his wife and still follow the law. Rather than embracing marriage and the woman they had once loved, men abused this law and their hearts became harder. Jesus made perfectly clear that the law given by Moses was designed to protect women from a life of bondage at the mercy of hard-hearted men. This fits the theme of their questions, "How much can we get away with?"

Pitting Jesus against Moses was the best religious leaders could do to try to trap Jesus. He was supposed to follow them, their traditions, their rules, their god. Jesus, God in skin, declared, "Before Abraham was, 'I am," (John 8:58). This statement infuriated the religious leaders and hardened their hearts further toward Christ. God worked His plan of redemption through the hard hearts and evil ways of the people appointed to be ambassadors of God. God's holy plan included the suffering, death and resurrection of His Son for the redemption of His people. God's plan was carried out through the hard hearts of the religious leaders.

Contrast Jesus' interactions with the hard-hearted religious leaders and His interactions with the broken-hearted. To one group He pressed harder and challenged more; to the other group Jesus invited people to rise up in hope and trust in Him.

The common thread in Jesus' work with hard-hearted or broken-hearted people is that He worked in and through both. The hard-hearted became more stubborn and the evil in their hearts became more evident. They spread evil through their words and deeds and stirred up crowds against Jesus. The tender-hearted trusted Jesus, grew up in love and became more merciful toward themselves and others. The meek in heart spread the good news of hope in Christ's work with great fervor.

God works through all circumstances. Jesus alone, as redeemer, works in and through all life events to bring about his good and gracious will. He draws the faithful closer to Himself; He allows the hard hearted to continue in their ways. Hard-hearted stagnation, by its very nature, is movement away from Him. Jesus continues to call human beings to a life of love and mercy that He embodies. Hope and trust guide us into deeper faith, knowing that God works through all things for us and in us as He has done throughout time.

HOPE IN JESUS ONLY—THE SERMON ON THE MOUNT

Jesus, alone, can sit on a mountain and proclaim himself the promised one of Israel, the Messiah. Jesus speaks a litany of "blessed are you" statements known as the beatitudes. These statements of Jesus reveal who He is and who those redeemed to follow Him are through Him. The beatitudes are a call to grow in faith and love. Jesus expounds on God's laws, making them absolute, leaving no room to be anything less than perfect.

This led to Jesus' statement that He came to fulfill the whole law perfectly, not to abolish the law (see Matthew 5:17).

Jesus' sermon must be taken in context, as a whole, as the sermon through which He reveals Himself as the One in whom we are invited to place our hope, the only way to life and life eternal. Jesus addresses a long list of topics coupling them with the demand, "You therefore must be perfect, as your heavenly Father is perfect," (Matthew 5:48). Jesus demanded perfect obedience of His listeners, perfection even above the letter of the law. Here are some of the topics Jesus addressed: anger, lust, divorce, oaths, retaliation, loving enemies, giving to the needy, fasting, laying up treasures in heaven, anxiousness, judging others, praying, and false prophecy. Here are Jesus' commands regarding adultery and divorce.

"Jesus declared, 'You have heard that it was said, you shall not commit adultery. But I say to you that everyone who looks at a woman with lustful intent has already committed adultery with her in his heart,'" (Matthew 5:27-28). The full intent of God's law commanding all to "not commit adultery" was to keep the heart pure for relationship with God, spouse and others. Simply looking at another with lustful intent was named as adultery by Christ. After making perfectly clear God's absolute demand, Jesus ushers in this demand, "It was also said, 'Whoever divorces his wife, let him give her a certificate of divorce.' But I say to you that everyone who divorces his wife, except on the ground of sexual immorality, makes her commit adultery, and whoever marries a divorced woman commits adultery," (Matthew 5:31-32).

Jesus leaves no room for lessening the law or playing religion with it. Perfection was Christ's demand in the Sermon on the Mount! Impossible was the cry of the people on that day and impossible is our cry. The absolute truth is that it is completely impossible to fulfill the law. Christ alone fulfills what He demands! We hope in Christ alone who said, "With man this is impossible, but with God all things are possible," (Matthew 19:26). Jesus also invited, "Come to me, all who labor and are heavy laden, and I will give you rest," (Matthew 11:28). Jesus spoke the whole truth of the law that could only be followed perfectly by Him, through his life and ultimate ransom sacrifice. Matthew recorded, "When Jesus finished these sayings, the crowds were astonished at his teaching, for he was teaching them as one who had authority, and not as their scribes," (Matthew 7:28-29).

Jesus' statements about divorce, quoted out of context, apart from the whole of His sermon on the mountain, have caused great harm in the hearts and lives of broken people. Using Jesus' words against tenderhearted people strips the very hope Jesus lived, died, and rose again to win on behalf of and provide to the brokenhearted. The harm done by misuse must not be understated nor should it be tolerated.

The proper use of Christ's words leads to these important questions: Where do these words of Christ leave broken-hearted people? Where do these words of Christ leave those who have divorced for reasons other than adultery? Where do Christ's words leave those who have been divorced and those who have remarried? The hope-filled answer for all people is, always and only, at Christ's mercy. He is our Savior. Christ delights in ushering light and life into the darkest places. We cry out to Christ in hope and faith, trusting that He delights in fulfilling His promises to us, and in us.

Jesus, the long-awaited Savior, alone, has the power and authority to free people who had been separated from God. Our hope is in Christ alone, who frees us for a life of freedom. He accomplished this by placing Himself in a position of bondage, as a prisoner, in the hands of those who committed adultery against Him and in violent anger crucified Him. Christ accomplished redemption, setting us free, by taking into His very life the sin that would enslave us, both our own sin as well as the sin of those who sin against us. Christ's life is the ransom for our lives, giving us hope and freedom.

CHAPTER 5

Freedom

What is freedom? What is freedom in the context of our lives or the lives of those we love, as divorced human beings? As we wrestle with the concept of freedom in our lives, we will address the freedom Christ desires for us and won for us. We will also address the question, "How does Christ free us?" Prior to addressing freedom in Christ, we need to delve into an honest discussion about what happens to our hearts and lives when we choose not to or are unable to live in freedom.

MISSING OR MISUSING FREEDOM

When we live apart from freedom, we miss life and living. Sadly, many live robotically apart from breath and life, bound to a life of captivity. Here is one example: from one Sunday morning to the next, people sit in sanctuaries hearing that they are sinners, and because Jesus died on the cross they are forgiven and have eternal life. Many leave the sanctuary only to step into unhealthy homes of adultery, disrespect, rage, hatred, gossip, stealing, and overall misuse of the gift of life. Hypocrisy flourishes. Children watch hypocrisy; and confused by hypocrisy, they become angry at inconsistencies. Generation after generation arrogantly believe they have license to sin against others because Jesus forgives them. The Scriptures, prayer, and praise become narrowed to a Sunday morning rote exercise that leads to complacency -- horrible misuse of the gifts of God.

"Honor your father and mother," (Exodus 20:12) is demanded of children apart from God's word, "Fathers, do not provoke your children to anger, but bring them up in the discipline and instruction of the Lord," (Ephesians 6:4). "Wives submit to your husbands," (Ephesians 5:22) is commanded apart from Paul's call, "submit one to another out of reverence for Christ," and "husbands love your wives as Christ loved the church and gave himself up for her," (Ephesians 5:25). It is better to give than to receive serves as a law unto itself, apart from a necessary understanding that one consistent, powerful theme in the Scriptures is that receiving is one of the highest forms of giving.

Other-care trumps self-care, rather than properly seeing both as God's high calling. We may not have been taught or truly grasped hold of God's desire that our individual human life is to be treated as a holy gift to be handled with great mercy and love. We may seek the self-care we need through caring for and giving to others. Living to get self-care by giving to others what we need is a bottomless pit. Bottomless pits lead to anger.

"Anger is wrong" was boldly stated in my childhood home. I watched anger, I questioned anger, and I became angry that the anger I felt was not allowed to be expressed. I developed an internal sense of being wrong for feeling anger. I have since learned that anger expressed in respectful love is a healthy, necessary part of living life fully alive. Rage expressed through a violent temper, for example, disrespects life and is an enemy of freedom.

There are church and home environments that teach, either intentionally or unintentionally, that emotions are an enemy of freedom. Rather than being cherished as a gift from God and masterfully existing side by side with head knowledge, emotions are suppressed and even denied. Knowledge and the "truth" of God's word can become a hiding place and sadly, may even be elevated to the position of an altar upon which God-given emotions are sacrificed.

Feeling feelings becomes horribly uncomfortable and often leads to feeding emotions. Under eating or overeating, misuse of alcohol, drugs, and/or sex is widespread. Pornography, a hopeless replacement for true intimacy, is rampant. Many who partake in the online world are riddled with guilt, yet hopeless to stop the adultery of this addiction. Others feel no guilt at all in the use of modern technology in the privacy of their own homes or offices. Shame leads to silence, lack of guilt leads to arrogance. Integration of the whole being is forfeited for compartmentalized living that leads to depression and a long litany of health issues.

Deep relationships where true matters of the heart and challenging conversations can be discussed, apart from judgment, may not exist. In that event, the human heart is stifled in silence. Somewhere, sometime in this silence, a detrimental set of internal principles are learned. Our belief in our values comes to be determined by our achievements or our work. We became human doings, caught in a vicious cycle of trying to be enough to meet our own expectations and the expectations of others. Simply being a human being became painful and true rest unknown. We cry out in expectant hope, there must be more!

FREEDOM IN CHRIST

Freedom in Christ comes by receiving and trusting Christ at His word. He perfectly binds us to Himself for a life of freedom. Only in Him can we find value that cannot be defined narrowly in our own mind or by those around us. Understanding our value as human beings to the One who created our lives for living is a hallmark of freedom. In the knowledge of our value to our Creator, everything we do flows from our being. We are human beings, not human doings. We are a holy creation set free to be. There is no freedom to be found when what we do drives our belief in our value as a human being. Our activity and actions must appropriately flow from freedom.

Picture a newborn baby. Babies are free to simply be and loved just because they are breathing. They can only receive. God's design teaches us that whether a newborn or on our death bed, only able to receive, we have value. God's design also teaches us that while we are healthy, able, and strong, the fruit of our lives flows from our position of being, a position of freedom.

My vineyard continues to teach me about freedom. I am a branch of the one true vine, grafted into Christ, the True Vine. Christ's desire for us is to live the life and freedom He won for us. Freedom flows naturally from a relationship in Christ. Here are some examples that urge us to keep our focus on freedom. Christ feeds our hearts with His Word, like the leaves taking in the light and converting it to energy. By His Spirit He keeps us, like the Band-aid® holds the bud in the vine. He challenges us to grow in faith and trust, like the vine yielding to the hand of the gardener. His blood, like the sap flow of the vine, cleanses every cell in our body both from our own sin and from the sin others have committed against us. He is the bread of life and living water, supplying nutrients, and quenching our thirst like the roots of the vine to the branches.

CHRIST'S WORK USHERING IN FREEDOM

The following stories illustrate Christ's work in the lives of the people bound by a plethora of issues—illness, misused religion, and shame. In each story and in all stories of Christ's work, Jesus sets human beings free. Christ flips common practice upside down as He displays His magnificent love for the humble in heart and puts to shame those who hold people captive. In freedom He called people to truly live a life of the freedom He won for them. His work then and His work now are the same work.

Christ saw human beings as valuable and of great worth simply because they were alive and breathing. He also knew their God-breathed need for freedom in His life. He didn't love them because of their stature, their health, or their knowledge. He didn't love them because of their statistics. Astoundingly, Jesus touched these supposedly untouchable human beings to heal them and bring them life. Jesus defended them from those who would keep them bound. Jesus also shattered the notion that the Sabbath day laws and rules prohibited the work of God in the lives of human beings.

Prior to diving into these stories, please ponder Christ's work in general. Christ's word and work freed all aspects of a human being for life both in the present and for all eternity. This fact must not be understated. When Christ freed an individual, freedom occurred in the present, for the present and for all eternity. Many falsely attempt to make Christ's work only about freeing someone for eternal life that occurs someday when a person dies. This enslaves people, leaving little or no hope for freedom today. Any form of limiting Christ's work is misuse of God's gift of freedom in the life of His Son.

Another aspect of Christ's work is that redemption won by Christ freed the whole being—body, soul, mind, heart, and spirit. The woman bound by disease and the man born blind needed Jesus' word and work in their lives to free them from that which kept them bound. Jesus healed them. Healing indicated making an individual whole in the very life of Christ for freedom and continued life, health and aliveness in Him. Healing an illness or blindness or making the deaf hear was only one aspect of the whole work of Christ in the lives of human beings. I've chosen these stories because of their particular meaning for me, but all stories of Christ's work fit under these general statements. Please join me as we place ourselves into Christ's story as He walked this earth.

Jesus approached a disabled woman. By both word and touch He freed her for freedom and life. As God, He could have spoken the word from a distance. Instead of keeping Himself in a sanitized bubble, He chose to touch a human being, a woman. He made Himself one with her, raising her up to a life of freedom. With his word and touch Jesus made this woman whole. She responded by glorifying God. Those around her rejoiced in Jesus' healing mercy.

> And behold, there was a woman who had had a disabling spirit for eighteen years. She was bent over and could not fully straighten herself. When Jesus saw her, he called her over and said to her, "Woman, you are freed (apoluō) from your disability." And he laid his hands on her, and immediately she was made straight, and she glorified God. But the ruler of the synagogue, indignant because Jesus had healed on the Sabbath, said to the people, "There are six days in which work ought to be done. Come on those days and be healed, and not on the Sabbath day." Then

> the Lord answered him, "You hypocrites! Does not each of you on the Sabbath untie his ox or his donkey from the manger and lead it away to water it? And ought not this woman, a daughter of Abraham whom Satan bound for eighteen years, be loosed from this bond on the Sabbath day?" As he said these things, all his adversaries were put to shame, and all the people rejoiced at all the glorious things that were done by him (Luke 13:11-17).

Notice that Jesus' word and work caused a greater divide between those who would receive Him, and the religious leaders who wanted Him stopped. Jesus' work shamed religious leaders and through shame their anger grew more intense, leading to a deeper desire to silence Christ. They ultimately imprisoned Jesus and crucified Him for freeing human beings for a life of freedom.

Jesus set another human being free as He journeyed on the dusty streets 2,000 years ago. He healed a man born blind. Again, we witness the Messiah speaking to and touching a human being in order to make them whole. We also see a great divide between those who received Jesus at His word and those who would keep people bound.

> As he passed by, he saw a man blind from birth. And his disciples asked him, "Rabbi, who sinned, this man or his parents, that he was born blind?" Jesus answered, "It was not that this man sinned, or his parents, but that the works of God might be displayed in him. We

> must work the works of him who sent me while it is day; night is coming, when no one can work. As long as I am in the world, I am the light of the world." Having said these things, he spit on the ground and made mud with the saliva. Then he anointed the man's eyes with the mud and said to him, "Go, wash in the pool of Siloam" (which means Sent). So he went and washed and came back seeing. Jesus heard that they had cast him out, and having found him he said, "Do you believe in the Son of Man?" He answered, "And who is he, sir, that I may believe in him?" Jesus said to him, "You have seen him, and it is he who is speaking to you." He said, "Lord, I believe," and he worshiped him (John 9:1-7, 35-38).

As we journey into the freedom Christ desires for and grants to individuals, we must pay close attention to the questions in John chapter 9. Jesus' disciples ask a very important question, "Who sinned that he was born blind?" Jesus answers, "It was not that this man sinned, or his parents, but that the works of God might be displayed in him" (John 9:2-3). Jesus' words help us understand that Jesus doesn't make the conversation with us about this sin or that sin or who was at fault. Jesus sees broken lives as an opportunity for God's work to be displayed. This question also gives us permission to ask Jesus hard questions without fear of rejection.

Religious leaders asked the healed man, "Then how were your eyes opened" (John 9:10)? Others asked, "How can a man who is a sinner [Jesus] do such signs" (John 9:16)? This helps us understand that some want freedom limited to their understanding or rules. They wanted people bound, not free in Christ.

Jesus asked the healed man, "Do you believe in the Son of Man" (John 9:35)? Jesus gave the formerly blind man an opportunity to see who had healed him. The man eagerly asked, "Who is he that I may believe in him" (John 9:36)? Jesus said to him, "You have seen him, and it is he who is speaking to you" (John 9:37). The freed man replied, "'Lord, I believe' and he worshiped him" (John 9:38). Worship of Jesus took place right then and there as Jesus revealed Himself to the healed man, giving us profound insight into freedom's relationship to worshiping Christ. Jesus frees; we worship.

These questions led me to ask hard questions of myself as I meditated on the fact that while my heart was beating, my lungs breathing and my mind working, I was not living in freedom. I was dying the slow death of depression and shame. I asked myself, "What am I blind to?" I also asked, "What do I want Jesus to do for me?" I pictured Jesus raising me up, healing my blindness, my illness, while calling me to live life. Jesus called me into a relationship of freedom in Him and out of the religion I was stuck in.

Jesus urged me to trust and granted me the courage to trust that His word was for me as I placed myself in these stories. My internal belief that I was untouchable and unworthy was being slowly shattered as Jesus reached out and touched me. He called me forth from the tomb, from blindness, from illness into freedom. Relationship with the risen Lord breeds health—healthy relationships and healthy living. Paul calls those who have been freed by Christ to live alive in the freedom won by Christ. "For you were called to freedom, brothers. Only do not use your freedom as an opportunity for the flesh, but through love serve one another. For the whole law is fulfilled in one word: 'You shall love your neighbor as yourself'" (Galatians 5:13-14).

LIVING IN FREEDOM—LOVING SELF AND NEIGHBOR

Loving one's neighbor is widely preached and taught to all ages. While it is true and right to love our neighbor, there is much more to living. Loving one's self must also be practiced. Loving self, as Paul said in the verse above, is the platform for loving others. In Christ, loving both self and others unselfishly is redemption living and breeds freedom. Christ's love drives unselfish love of ourselves that leads to a healthy love for our neighbor. Loving ourselves, that is, taking care of ourselves as whole human beings, is a critical aspect of the fruit of living. Apart from deeply caring for our lives, we are only capable of shallow love for our neighbor. We must care for ourselves in order to care for others.

Loving ourselves means understanding that our needs are God-given and worthy of our attention. We need proper nutrition for our body, and we need to feed our soul, heart, mind, and spirit with proper nutrition. Here are some of our needs. We have a need to be loved and cherished, for who we are, as a valuable creation of God. We have a need for emotional and physical safety. We have a need to be heard.

Our human needs mirror our need for God. This is God's design, so that we will want Him and seek him more. Ponder these important parallels to these additional needs. We need nutrition; Jesus is the bread of life. We need water; He is living water. Our life needs more life and freedom; Christ is the resurrection and life. We breathe; He is the breath of life. Our body cleanses us from toxic poisons through our blood, liver, kidneys, heart, and lungs; His blood cleanses us from the poison of sin and death. Understanding these parallels drives us to take care of ourselves so that we live in freedom and hope as God designed.

Beginning to understand the spiritual parallels to my life, I grew in freedom. I learned to value my life and speak out when being hurt. As I grew, I learned that living in freedom must include healthy boundaries. I put into practice what I was learning from authors Dr. Henry Cloud and Dr. John Townsend (see *Boundaries: When to Say Yes, How to Say No To Take Control of Your Life:* Cloud, H. and Townsend, J. Zondervan Publishing, 2017.) After years of growth and my journey into self-care, I developed the voice to ask for help, a voice that had been silenced over the years. Unhealthy thoughts of, I can do it myself, had reigned powerfully in my mind.

Receiving the truth of God's desire for freedom, for me, led to speaking the truth in love in my home to my spouse. Changing the culture of self-care in my heart and mind led to a change in the culture of my home. In love and mercy, I spoke my needs for calm and safety. When that request was not met, I moved out of my home to create separation. After a painful time of observation, discernment and prayer, I asked for a divorce. Through self-care and developing a voice to speak my needs, brokenness took place, and through it, I experienced freedom. Freedom in Christ freed me to live a life of greater love and mercy for myself and for those around me. Freedom in Christ also led to deeper intimacy with Christ and those around me, even as I embarked on living life as a single woman.

CHAPTER 6

Intimacy

God created all people with a deep need for intimacy and an inherent desire for intimacy. Freeing human beings for intimacy is an aspect of God's remarkable work of redemption. Is intimacy possible from our place in life as a divorced person? Sexual intimacy may be the first thought to come to mind and we might quickly answer, no. The answer, however is a resounding, yes! There is so much more to intimacy and to God's design for redemption, hope, and healing. God never leaves us lacking. Embracing our needs and desires as a gift from God, a mirror of his desire for intimacy with us, is our path for this chapter.

One of the most beautiful forms of intimacy takes place when a mother nurses her baby. Skin on skin and eye to eye contact between baby and mother is the foundational relationship upon which all other intimacy is built. The key elements of intimacy in that earliest relationship are trust and vulnerability. Babies are completely vulnerable and must trust that the mother or another caregiver will be there to meet their need for closeness and food. Notice that I list food after closeness. Both are necessary but closeness and trust are the nutrition one needs to feed intimacy and nurture vulnerability. Closeness, intimacy, and vulnerability, as well as food, must all be considered primary benefits of that mother and child relationship.

As a child grows up and no longer nurses, closeness and trust remain because mother and baby have bonded. Meeting one's need for closeness and food takes on different forms with both mother and father, such as snuggling, skin contact through touch, and conversation around the family table. The need for rich intimacy and a place to be vulnerable continues through the need for heart to heart conversation. This provides the growing individual opportunity to fully express themselves in a relationship of trust where they can be vulnerable, naked in a sense, and not ashamed. The powerful need for intimacy with Christ and other humans is designed by God to be met in the home with open conversation and genuine concern for the whole being. The blessings of having an intimate, strong bond with mother and father must not be underestimated as the all-important foundation upon which one enters into a marriage relationship.

The marriage relationship closely mirrors God's intimate relationship with human beings. We were created in God's image for intimacy, closeness, trust, vulnerability, and nakedness without shame. Sexual expression in intimacy between husband and wife reflects God's relationship with his people, a masterful design of life breeding life. A mom feeding her baby with milk from her body includes the intrinsic benefits of intimacy such as safety, closeness, and touch, as well as a plethora of other complex needs. God designed human beings so that sexuality and sex affect all aspects of our complex being. Pleasure is part, but certainly not the whole, as husband and wife engage in sexual expression apart from shame.

The possibilities for breeding intimacy are endless in a one-flesh relationship that is grounded in trust, closeness, and vulnerability. One example of God's creative work is God's design of the human body. He designed humans for making love. Ponder the difference between all animals and human beings. Animals copulate while the female is ovulating in order to continue the species; human beings make love. In human love-making there is opportunity to create life as well as to create more love. God created the human body to breed more love as two people experience sexual intimacy with one another.

God's gift of Eve to Adam as his partner and soul-mate was a holy gift for a high purpose. God instructed Adam and Eve, "Be fruitful, multiply and fill the earth" (Genesis 1:28). God ordained their marriage with these words, "Therefore a man shall leave his father and his mother and hold fast to his wife, and they shall become one flesh. And the man and his wife were both naked and were not ashamed," (Genesis 2:24-25). Husband and wife were naked before God and one another, vulnerable and in a position of pure trust. They were not ashamed.

Relationships between mom and child may not have included an intimate bonding. Sadly, parents and child may not continue developing intimacy, or perhaps intimacy was never there to begin with. Intimacy will likely be sought after in less than healthy ways. With no early roadmap for intimacy, trust, safety, and vulnerability, individuals often embark on exploring their sexuality with their peer group or in privacy through the online world, believing they will fulfill their most basic need for intimacy by engaging in sexual activity. For so many, the sexual relationship with a spouse or former spouse bred neither intimacy nor life. This is a profound source of deep pain in an individual's heart. We must engage in a frank discussion of that pain by naming the many enemies of intimacy.

ENEMIES OF INTIMACY

Adam and Eve give us an example of trust going awry, and a list of enemies of intimacy because of their disobedience to God's design and command. "And the Lord God commanded the man, saying, 'You may surely eat of every tree of the garden, but of the tree of the knowledge of good and evil you shall not eat, for in the day that you eat of it you shall surely die,'" (Genesis 2:16-17). They chose to place themselves above God's command and they ate from that tree. Rather than living in God's design, in freedom, Adam and Eve chose to disobey. Their very first sin led to shame; shame led to hiding their nakedness and hiding from God. Shame also led to anger, and anger led to blaming God, the serpent and each other. Trust was not present and they lost their innocence. "God asked, 'Who told you you were naked? Have you eaten of the tree of which I commanded you not to eat?'" (Genesis 3:11)? Adam and Eve provide us a short list of enemies of intimacy: shame, hiding, and blame.

Intimacy has many other enemies. Naming the enemies will help us understand the challenges associated with experiencing true intimacy as well as understand the painful internal battle that rages in many broken human hearts. Naming the enemies of intimacy also brings issues into the light and allows God to work through our deep brokenness. Enemies include but are not limited to anger at others, anger at ourselves, lack of trust, fear of being vulnerable, and lies. Selfishness is a powerful enemy of intimacy. Tragically and sadly, many men and women have been deeply wounded by the selfishness of others who misuse God's great gift. Emotional withdrawal of one or both individuals is an enemy of intimacy.

One of the greatest enemies of intimacy is abuse, abuse of any kind, that includes domination of one person over another. This leads to intimacy being corrupted. Domination takes place in many harmful ways. The most detrimental to the heart and soul happens when one human being takes advantage of another human being sexually. These types of offenses affect the whole human being—body, heart, soul, mind, and spirit. The ability to trust and be vulnerable can be lost because of these violations.

For many, deep wounds began to form early in life as they witnessed their parents' discomfort with their own sexuality.

That discomfort led to painful silence, with little or no conversation about sex or sexuality taking place in the home or church. Children are often left to their own discovery, trapped in a world where there is no one to trust with their most personal thoughts and deep pain. Perhaps unintentionally, but nonetheless sadly, children are shamed into silence.

In other cases, children silently and helplessly watch abuse take place in their own homes. Dignity, respect, trust, vulnerability, and openness are not modeled. Children observe domination, sarcasm, confusion, fear, and shame. Often drugs or alcohol are used and abused in conjunction with abuse in a flailing attempt to mask deep pain. This leaves a huge empty place in the hearts and minds of children, the very hearts and minds God designed to be filled by intimacy and trust.

Children and young adults often seek to meet their needs for intimacy through sexual activity. Emotionally immature human beings in adult bodies explore and express their sexuality through sex, casually and without an awareness of the damage being caused. Unaware that they are seeking intimacy, they misuse freedom. The pleasure of the moment, a sad substitute for love and intimacy, drives activity in relationships. Pleasure leads to bondage and pain. Numb to pain, they become numb to their internal world and remain in a confusing, vicious cycle. Activity where intimacy is sought through sex is confusing and damaging to the soul.

Sexual experiences of many broken hearted, hurting human beings include, but are not limited to, the following enemies of intimacy: pornography, casual sex, hooking up for sex, social media sex, phone sex and sexting. Sexual abuse may also include verbal, emotional, and physical abuse, all of which are enemies of intimacy. Various forms of sexual abuse include but are not limited to: dominance, violent sex, rape, sodomy, and bondage. The one who dominates as the offender battles one type of war, the one who is offended battles a very different internal war. All activity where intimacy is sought through sex and the misuse of sex is confusing and damaging to the soul.

Verbal, sexual, physical, and emotional abuse of children are enemies of intimacy. We'd like to believe child abuse isn't rampant, but it takes place in epidemic proportions. Abuse of children takes place in the homes of those who attend church and in the homes of those who do not attend church. It takes place in homes where people say they believe in Christ as well as in homes where people don't profess faith in Christ. Adults charged with caring for children misuse their power, and bring great harm to all aspects of a developing human being. Children are confused and trapped in the belief they are at fault for the violation of their being. Shame and silence become a way of life as one tries to make sense of external and internal chaos.

Marriage is often entered into from these painful life experiences. For a time, these experiences can be ignored. Eventually pain surfaces, generally with a vengeance. These painful life experiences breed war on the soul and spirit, heart, and mind. They can also breed pain in the human body, either through chronic pain or illness. Meant by God's design to live in freedom and intimacy, the human being is bound in pain and shame. The pain and shame continue in the deathly silence of a culture uncomfortable even to speak about sexuality.

Intimacy, safety, and freedom—do we dare to hope that these aspects of life are even a remote possibility for deeply wounded hearts? Can Christ work healing in the midst of such pain and shame? Can Christ free a human being from such a war on the soul? The answer is a resounding YES. Christ's work can and does set one free to be fully human and fully alive! Redemption of the whole human being—heart, mind, spirit, soul, and body, is the work of Christ as he frees us for intimacy.

Professional help goes hand in hand with the healing God desires and works for those who suffer great pain from abuse and any forms of enemies of intimacy. Very complex issues such as attachment and bonding, trust issues, a deep belief that one is at fault for the abuse they endured, etc., are present. Developing a trustworthy relationship with a therapist, counselor or support group creates a place where one learns proper boundaries as well as to be vulnerable in a safe environment.

FREEDOM FOR INTIMACY

Freedom for true intimacy is possible. God seeks us out and gives us courage to find places of safety. Safety breeds trust and provides space to be vulnerable. We need to be seen and known as human beings, fully alive from the context of integrating all of our life experiences. God calls us out of silence and shame, into the beauty of trust and openness. Where can that relationship be found? Men and women alike are called into the gracious arms and life of the Redeemer, Christ Himself. Our one-flesh, intimate position of being grafted into Christ's holy life, is the context for all intimacy. Intimacy in Christ breeds life by his creation and continued re-creation. All aspects of human life—body, heart, soul, emotions, mind, and spirit—are safely redeemed in Christ's life for a life of intimacy and freedom.

Freedom in Christ is a reality in our lives. Living in that reality, in the midst of our brokenness, needs a daily, even moment by moment, choice to fix our eyes on hope. We must fix our eyes on Jesus. Scripture says, "By his wounds we are healed" (1 Peter 2:24). Healed, yet broken, we are courageous to ask for help with the very complex wounds with which we live. We must look at the past, not to stay there, but to understand where intimacy was lost and why we might continue hurtful patterns of seeking intimacy where it cannot be found. Our wounds are real, but our wounds do not define us; freedom in Christ defines us.

We need to reach out for help to counselors or therapists through whom God works to help free us for intimacy, out of the bondage of pain and brokenness. We are called to pray for healthy relationships with other human beings who will cherish our lives and our stories. We slowly build those relationships of trust without misusing any aspect of life including our sexuality or sex. From that healthy position, we cling to God's word and trust God's word to heal our broken hearts.

The Apostle Paul, a single man, knew rich intimacy and freedom in Christ. He not only knew rich intimacy, he was inspired by God to write profound words relating to intimacy, marriage, and healthy relationships. Reflect on these intimate words Paul declared, "There is one body and one Spirit—just as you were called to the one hope that belongs to your call— one Lord, one faith, one baptism, one God and Father of all, who is over all and through all and in all," (Ephesians 4:4-5). This oneness in Christ and in the Spirit of the living God, breeds intimacy and life.

Paul called freed human beings out of silence with these words, "Speaking the truth in love, we are to grow up in every way into him who is the head, into Christ, from whom the whole body, joined and held together by every joint with which it is equipped, when each part is working properly, makes the body grow so that it builds itself up in love," (Ephesians 4:15-16). In genuine love, Paul called human beings to "put off your old self, that belongs to your former manner of life and is corrupt through deceitful desires, and to be renewed in the spirit of your minds, and to put on the new self, created after the likeness of God in true righteousness and holiness," (Ephesians 4:22-24).

God created life with great capacity for healing. The breath of God breathes life into the depth of our brokenness, healing us on a cellular level. Christ's life breeds righteousness and holiness for intimate living in Him and with one another. The healing love of Christ is to be mirrored in all relationships. If safety, hope, and freedom are not present, we must create healthy boundaries. If that is not possible, we must remove ourselves from those relationships. This healing action may not feel loving and merciful, but God's word calls us to speak a loud NO to any type of relationship that does not breed safety, vulnerability, and intimacy.

Freedom for intimacy is designed by God to be the marriage relationship between one man and one woman for a life together. God designed marriage to be life that breeds life. Redemption freedom takes place within the safety of the intimacy that is created through love and respect. Growing in intimacy takes place through experiencing one another in every way, connecting physically, emotionally, spiritually, while cherishing the beautiful as well as the broken pieces.

CHRIST'S INTIMACY WITH HIS BRIDE, A MIRROR

Paul's call for intimacy through physical oneness in marriage mirrors Christ's relationship with and desire for intimacy with His body, the church. By church Paul means those redeemed, set free in Christ, by His ransom (lutron), His atoning sacrifice. In a powerful litany, Paul unfolds two types of relationships wherein intimacy is central to life and freedom—the oneness of Christ with His bride and the mirroring life-giving oneness in the marriage of husband and wife. Paul flows back and forth between the two in poetic beauty.

These words are a call to beautiful intimacy in Christ for all people in whatever state in life: single, married, widowed, or divorced. These words are also a call to husbands and wives for the life-breeding rich intimacy in marriage. In light of intimacy and redemptive freedom, ponder Paul's words,

> Giving thanks always and for everything to God the Father in the name of our Lord Jesus Christ, submitting to one another out of reverence for Christ. Wives, submit to your own husbands, as to the Lord. For the husband is the head of the wife even as Christ is the head of the church, his body, and is himself its Savior. Now as the church submits to Christ, so also wives should submit in everything to their husbands. Husbands, love your wives, as Christ loved the church and gave himself up for her, that he might sanctify her, having cleansed her by the washing of water with the word, so that he might present the church to himself in splendor, without spot or wrinkle or any such thing, that she might be holy and without blemish. In the same way husbands should love their wives as their own bodies. He who loves his wife loves himself. For no one ever hated his own flesh, but nourishes and cherishes it, just as Christ does the church, because we are members of his body. "Therefore a man shall leave his father and mother and hold fast to his wife, and the two shall become one flesh." This mystery is profound, and I am saying that it refers to Christ and the church. However, let each one of you love his wife as himself, and let the wife see that she respects her husband (Ephesians 5:20-33).

The fluid nature of Paul's words flows from the perspective of intimacy, life, and freedom won by Christ. This intimacy is expressed in and through Christ and the church as well as in marriage between husband and wife. The profound mystery of which Paul speaks is the life-breeding intimacy of the one-flesh relationship between Christ and His bride. Oneness is for the purpose of pro-creation in every possible way. God creates life by his oneness with mankind; husbands and wives create life by their oneness. Life breeds life.

Paul calls both husband and wife to submit to one another. Submitting one to another in the context of emotional and physical safety breeds life. Submission provides a safe place in which to be vulnerable. Husbands, loving wives as Christ loved the church and gave Himself up for her, breeds freedom, and leaves no room for selfish or abusive behavior. Wives submitting to loving trustworthy husbands as to Christ breeds freedom and trust for both husband and wife. Christ never took advantage of a single soul, but rather cherished and raised them up to life, hope, and freedom.

Redemption intimacy breeds freedom to live life in honest, genuine care and concern for one's own life and the life of others. Marriage is designed to be a place of safety and rest, just as safety and rest is God's desire for His church. Mercy and love reign and continue to grow in the pure pleasure and fulness of human expression. Through intimate expression of love in the marriage bed, husbands and wives live out the profound truth expressed earlier, "receiving is one of the highest forms of giving." Giving flows from receiving in the profound gift of intimacy.

In a very different way, the same holds true for single individuals. Intimacy with Christ breeds life from a position of safety and rest. By God's design for life breeding life, intimate expression of our lives in the love relationship with Christ, we live out this profound truth: receiving is one of the highest forms of giving. Giving flows from receiving. Singleness includes a holy waiting, resting in the fulness of intimacy with Christ in rich trust, vulnerability and nakedness before him.

Intimacy with Christ and freedom in Christ drives the expression of one's sexuality or one's holy waiting. Oneness in Christ is designed to fill our greatest need for freedom and intimacy. God's design is corrupted when our hunger for intimacy drives us to seek intimacy through sex alone, by and for itself. Either sexual expression or holy waiting flow from our lives as we rest in an intimate position of oneness with Christ.

CHAPTER 7

Redeemed From, Through AND For

My study of the Greek words and my search of the Scriptures under the theme of redemption, revealed time and again the very simple words, from, through, and for. There is a circular, fluid relationship between these important words. These redemption concepts, from, through, and for are not linear like a tight rope or rigid like a rock path. During chaos and often even in life itself, many prefer a set of directions with step one, step two and step three; an instruction manual or a list of rules to follow. Life is not that way; marriage and divorce are certainly not that way. These three small words can serve as journey map, a simple way of thinking about our story and God's work in and through our story.

Divorced human beings have endured significant trauma of heart, soul, mind, and spirit. Broken human beings, all human beings, need Christ's redemption healing in order to live life in hope and freedom in Christ. Divorced human beings are no exception, but in fact are in dire need of Christ's redemptive work. One of the many challenges we face in the healing process is that every individual's story of trauma involving marriage and divorce is different.

Sadly, we don't know each other's stories because we've been silenced in shame, either by our own thinking or by the demand's others place on us to be silent. I've learned that while each story of the brokenness of a marriage and each divorce is different, there are many aspects of the story we share. Silence must end. We must bury our shame in Christ's tomb and rise to new life with Him. Our resurrection stories of courage and hope will help others in the journey of growing in redemption freedom. I've witnessed in myself and others that in the journey of life. one of the greatest challenges is to rise up out of silence, shame, and despair into hope and healing. I've slowly learned that when I tell my story in safe places, people don't judge me or reject me because of my divorce. Unfolding my story to the proper people with the perspective of courage, hope, and redemption in the midst of pain gives others opportunity to love me more. A safe place to tell our stories leads to vulnerability, and that leads to trusting and trust leads to intimacy.

REDEMPTION FROM

What are divorced human beings redeemed, released or freed from? The immediate, most visible aspect of being freed is freedom from one's spouse. Freedom from the chaos of the breakdown of the home cannot be ignored. With time, as the shock and pain subside, there are many other aspects one has the opportunity to be released from and freed from.

Being freed *from* believing that asking for help is a sign of weakness was a huge hurdle for me. "I can do this myself" slowly melted into "asking for help is an act of great courage." The courage to tell the truth about the pain I was in came slowly. Of course, I didn't outright lie, I was trying to look at my spouse and my marriage with hope and optimism. I had created a belief system where if I just worked harder our marriage would be ok. We were not ok, and I asked for help, slowly being freed *from* silence.

Being freed *from* fear of condemnation took place slowly too. I had been so focused on what others thought about me that I hadn't developed and matured the internal skill of thinking about how I think. The condemnation I thought others were thinking really stemmed from my own internal condemnation. Being set free *from* self-condemnation is a slower process yet, that continues today as I wrestle with being divorced, and the many complicated, associated issues of living single.

Freedom *from* taking responsibility for another human being's hurtful words and actions was a giant step in my growth. Slowly I relinquished the unhealthy belief that I had the duty to bear the whole load of our marriage and the whole load of our divorce. Paul's words issue the call to understand that we must take responsibility for self and allow others to be responsible for themselves. We must distinguish between burden and load, "Bear one another's burdens, and so fulfill the law of Christ. For if anyone thinks he is something, when he is nothing, he deceives himself. But let each one test his own work, and then his reason to boast will be in himself alone and not in his neighbor. For each will have to bear his own load," (Galatians 6:2-5). I had gotten this concept very mixed up, and I was slowly freed *from* the responsibility of bearing another person's load, that is something only they can do.

Redemption *from* the belief that my life didn't have value apart from my marriage was a turning point in my healing journey. My marriage defined me, as did my internal belief that I was a failure, because I couldn't make my marriage work. Slowly, through personal work with a Christian therapist, I broke away *from* the harsh belief system that my value was earned by my success. Freedom *from* those thoughts came through an understanding that God works redemption in all things, including my divorce. Slowly, piece by piece, I learned that rather than being a failure, speaking the truth in love was redemption coming to life in me, freeing me *from* despair.

Redemption *from,* in my particular story, included fleeing from rage and violence. I had convinced myself I could handle it and even deserved it. At first, I fled internally through depression and despair. I used unhealthy eating habits on both ends of the spectrum in a futile attempt to feed my need for safety and intimacy. I was freed *from* lack of self-care through an understanding that Christ is my rest and the bread of life for me. I fled *from* my home to seek proper care. Freed *from* danger, I am on the path of recovery, and even thrive in redemption's freedom.

REDEMPTION THROUGH

Redemption through Christ became a daily exercise for me as I placed myself into the stories of Jesus' walk on this earth. My self-defined failures melted into Christ's mercy and love as I meditated on these stories, allowing Christ to work through them for me. I visualized myself, like Lazarus, called forth from death into life. I was like Mary and Martha who questioned, "Lord, if you had been here our brother would not have died," (John 11:21, 32). Amazingly, Jesus didn't reject them for their cry of desperation. I wanted to be like the woman at the well. She loved that Jesus knew her whole story and was safe in his presence in full vulnerability and intimacy. Jesus' call to the disciples to follow him represented hope and freedom through movement and growth, as opposed to stagnation and death.

Redemption *through* Christ came as I visualized my life grafted into Christ's life, my home, where sap flows freely, bringing growth and healing. Rest became possible *through* visualizing myself as a branch in the True Vine. Picturing Christ's root and the root of the vines gave me stability when there was no security in my home life. Sap flow, growing, training, wounds being healed, pruning and the work of the gardener surrounded me in my vineyard. Growth took place through these vineyard and Scripture images.

Redemption hope and healing came *through* an intimate, vulnerable relationship with Christ. I begged Christ to heal my heart, emotions, soul, mind, spirit, and body as I rested "in" His life. I learned the role of human blood as it flows through one's entire body and how that important work related to Christ's blood flowing through the human body. Blood oxygenates—Christ, the breath of life, breathes life into our lives. Blood cleanses every cell—Christ's blood cleanses us in every way. White blood cells and platelets rush to a wound to heal; Christ's blood heals us. Blood pumps through the heart, the center of our being; Christ dwells in our heart through faith, pumping life through us. Blood flows at all times just as sap flows at all times; Christ is at work at all times in us.

Redemption flows *through* forgiveness and mercy. Receiving Christ's mercy freed me to be merciful toward myself. Christ's mercy toward me bred mercy in me toward others. Some relationships can be restored t*hrough* forgiveness, mutual respect, and love. Thank God when that takes place. Some relationships can't be restored and that is merciful too. Freedom *through* forgiveness takes place within the framework of healthy boundaries, that is, forgiving while not giving an individual opportunity to cause additional pain.

Paul's rich words call us into a deeper faith and understanding of the fulness of God's plan to work redemption (apolutrōsis) *through* the blood of Christ, "In him we have redemption *through* his blood, the forgiveness of our trespasses, according to the riches of his grace, which he lavished upon us, in all wisdom and insight making known to us the mystery of his will, according to his purpose, which he set forth in Christ as a plan for the fullness of time, to unite all things in him, things in heaven and things on earth," (Ephesians 1:7-10).

REDEMPTION FOR

What are divorced human beings, in fact all human beings, redeemed for? We are redeemed for relationship with God. God created Adam and Eve for intimate relationship with Him and with one another. They walked and talked with God, in complete nakedness before Him, and they were not ashamed. Shame and a plethora of other enemies of freedom, as we've discussed, became a powerful force when Adam and Eve turned from God in disobedience. Redemption (lutrosis) was necessary, and was fulfilled completely in Christ the ransom (lutron) for restoration of relationship between God and human beings. Christ, unlike Adam, obeyed the whole law perfectly, securing redemption.

We walk and talk with Christ, trusting Him, vulnerable and naked before Him, unashamed because of His life-creating life. We live *for* life, now in His life and for all eternity in His life. We are His bride, His friend, and His family. He pursues us as a passionate lover and calls us into that same passionate pursuit of Him. We live out our holy calling, receiving from Him the gifts he gives. Our life in Christ influences all aspects of life *for* relationship with one another.

Christ redeemed us *for* healthy relationships with one another. Redeemed by Christ, we are agents of His redeeming work in our relationships with one another. In the same manner, Christ places others in our lives to be agents of His redemption for us. Healthy relationships are the hallmark of a joy-filled, hope-filled life. Carefully, prayerfully we discern relationships that reflect safety, intimacy and rest for us. We spend our time and attention on fostering those relationships. At times we must end relationships with people whose lives do not breed life.

Christ redeemed us *for* worship. Worship is bowing before God as creator, and trusting him with our very being. Worship is thanking God, praising God, adoring God for His freeing work through His Son. Worship is receiving from God the gifts He delights in giving. He works redemption freedom; we worship. He heals our hearts; we worship. The apostle Paul calls our lives a living sacrifice, "I urge you, brothers and sisters, in view of God's mercy, to offer your bodies as a living sacrifice, holy and pleasing to God—this is your true and proper worship" (Romans 12:1, NIV).

The man born blind is a powerful story of *from, through,* and *for.* God freed a human being *from* blindness *through* Christ's word and touch, *for* worship. "Jesus heard that they had cast him out, and having found him he said, 'Do you believe in the Son of Man?' He answered, 'And who is he, sir, that I may believe in him?' Jesus said to him, 'You have seen him, and it is he who is speaking to you.' He said, 'Lord, I believe,' and he worshiped him" (John 9:35-38). Jesus received the healed man's worship. Like the healed man, we worship in spirit and in truth because we have received healing *from* Him, *through* Him, *for* worship of Him.

There is an additional aspect of the events in John 9 that informs our theme *from, through,* and *for.* Religious leaders had grand ideas of and strict demands for worship, that they attempted to impose on Jesus and the man Jesus healed. Jesus, in His mercy, called leaders *from* their rigid religious life, *through* the words of the healed man, *for* redemption freedom. They rejected Christ's call. They would have nothing to do with being called from their religious life by Jesus, whom they believed broke the laws of the Sabbath, or by a common man who had been blind from birth. *Through* the words of the healed man Jesus called out the blindness of religious leaders, *for* the further hardening of their hearts, *for* accomplishing God's redemption freedom (see John 9).

TRUST

God calls us to trust that He has redeemed, freed, and delivered us from, through, and for with the very life of His only Son. We trust that according to God's masterful design, redemption (lutrōsis) takes place in all aspects of our human life—heart, soul, mind, spirit, emotions, and body. Trust says, amen (so be it), in times of great pain and darkness; trust says, amen, as we learn to live in freedom. We say amen to God's work in all aspects of our being in every stage of our journey into wholeness.

Trusting God's work for us and in us explodes the walls of silence and shame, making room to receive more and more from Christ, who delights in giving. We embrace the journey of trusting that God's work *for* us and in us is for the purpose of working redemption *through* our stories of pain and divorce. The despair of trying to create a neat and tidy world gradually gives way to a beautifully messy world of trust, hope and healing.

Trusting Christ gives us a platform of freedom from which to love and trust other human beings, intimately, allowing ourselves to be vulnerable. Trusting Christ and others breeds healing and hope. Slowly isolation and silence give way to reaching out to others who will be kind and loving, consistent and truthful in relationship with us. As trust is built in relationships, we are provided a platform to live life freed *from* darkness that binds us, *through* God's redemption work, *for* a life of freedom.

CHAPTER 8

Letting Go

Letting go is an important aspect in the journey of Christ creating hope and healing. Letting go is a process of growth and maturity where we learn that releasing burdens makes room for healing. Letting go is a process that requires continual, intentional practice. As one practices letting go, room is made for healthy practices to fill the void created by releasing burdens.

Picture a person carrying big boulders in her arms, giant rocks that represent her burdens. She struggles under the weight, but in a comfortable sort of way because carrying burdens is more familiar than letting go. As she chooses to let go of her burdens, a weight is lifted and relief is felt. Relief may be short lived, however, because she doesn't know how to fill the void. As letting go of a burden is practiced, it becomes more familiar and comfortable.

Mary and Martha struggled with letting go of numerous giant boulders. Boulder number one, the Scriptures reveal, was their agonizing cry, "If you had been here our brother would not have died," (John 11:21, 32). Jesus did not chastise them for being bound to the past, He wept with them because of death, all death in general and the death of His dear friend Lazarus. Boulder number two was so big that when Jesus commanded, "take away the stone" all they could think about was the smell of death. Moments before Jesus had declared himself the Resurrection and the Life. Jesus said, you're correct, death stinks but don't let the smell keep you from seeing the resurrection possibilities in me, here and now. In faith, at Jesus' direction, they removed the stone and Jesus called the dead man to life. Boulder number three is revealed as their brother stood before them in grave clothes, fully bound. Jesus needed to instruct the sisters, "unbind (luō) him and let him go" (John 11:44). Their burdens kept them from seeing Lazarus' need for them to take action, to unbind him, so he could live his future with them.

Unbind him and let him go were Jesus' instruction to the people closest to Lazarus. The sisters of Lazarus had been helpless to heal their sick brother or raise their brother from death to life. Lazarus most certainly was unable to raise himself from the dead. They needed Jesus' work for them, to unbind them. Having been raised from the dead, Lazarus needed those around him to unbind him from the clothes of death. Letting go involves faith in Christ as well as the action of receiving and taking action. Letting go also includes the action of others around us, unbinding the clothes of death that bind us. The image of three heavy boulders will help us understand the challenges we face, and guide our discussion of the process of letting go.

BOULDER ONE: MISUSE OF THE WORD OF GOD

Boulder number one is the burden many hearts carry because God's word has been misused. The stink of death that misuse creates must be named and the stone rolled away. Jesus weeps at the death caused by the misuse of His word. We must acknowledge that whether intentional or unintentional, great harm has been caused by misuse. One particular chapter of the Bible, 1 Corinthians 7, will serve as the example for boulder one.

Paul's words to the new Christians in Corinth spoke into a culture in which people lived in one of the two extremes. Some viewed the body as unimportant to spiritual life, therefore one could, at a whim fulfill any desire for pleasure, even at another's expense, while still being faithful to God. Others believed that bodily urges should be subdued, even in marriage, for the purpose of a spiritual life. Spirituality was seen as separate from the physical body. Earthly relationships were viewed as trite and unimportant. Sexual activity apart from marriage, and sex with temple prostitutes, were rampant among these new Christians. With great urgency and intensity Paul said, wake up, time is short, Jesus is returning any moment (see 1 Corinthians 7:29). Paul's words reflect God's love for individuals in their present state, whether married, divorced, single, or widowed.

Paul wrote these words to the newly established church in Corinth, "To the married I give this charge (not I, but the Lord): the wife should not separate from her husband (but if she does, she should remain unmarried or else be reconciled to her husband), and the husband should not divorce his wife" (1 Corinthians 7:10-11). Paul's words, "not I, but the Lord" draw our attention back to Jesus' declaration that he did not come to abolish the law but to fulfill all of God's demands for righteousness.

Jesus words in the Sermon on the Mount, as we've discussed, made marriage between husband and wife absolute. He also made clear that any form of adultery, hatred, anger, lust, or misuse of His word would not be tolerated by God. Only at Christ's mercy can any and all people find hope and healing. The divorced, the married, the single, find mercy at his feet. Paul affirms and proclaims Christ's work when he declared to the people of Corinth, "And because of him you are in Christ Jesus, who became to us wisdom from God, righteousness and sanctification and redemption, so that, as it is written, "Let the one who boasts, boast in the Lord" (1 Corinthians 1:30-31).

Redemption (apolutrosis) means set free, delivered, and released. Christ is our Redemption, the One in whom we place our hope and trust, the One who provides healing. By His forgiveness Christ restored our relationship with God; by forgiveness Christ provides us life and a hope-filled opportunity to live our lives as His holy people. We live our lives by His Spirit in the holiness He won for us, honoring Him with our whole being as well as honoring Him through our relationships with others.

Boulder number one, the misuse of Scripture, is often forced on individuals living in dangerous homes. Individuals are told by religious leaders or an offending spouse that they must stay in the marriage, based on these verses in 1 Corinthians 7. Misuse of these verses' places additional boulders in the arms of people already carrying the weight of another's evil actions against them. Paul was talking about flippancy and arrogance toward marriage and sex, not dangerous living conditions.

Another form of this Scripture passage being used against a husband or wife takes place when the offending spouse breaks the marriage vows by adultery. Reconciliation is desirable and perhaps possible. At times it is not possible. There are times when reconciliation is forced upon a helpless person and accomplished by religious leaders or an offending spouse declaring, "You have to stay married or you're not a Christian, you have to forgive." A marriage may be saved but at the expense of placing heavy burdens on the heart and life of the offended. As discussed previously, Paul declared that marriage is to be a mutually loving, respectful commitment between husband and wife.

Boulder number one has been unduly placed upon many, because of this 1983 NIV translation of 1 Corinthians 7:27-28a, "Are you married? Do not seek a divorce. Are you unmarried? Do not look for a wife. But if you do marry, you have not sinned" (1 Corinthians 7:27-28a NIV). This poor translation gives the appearance that Paul is speaking to both married people and individuals who have never married. Many who have divorced and then married have carried the weight of this boulder of misuse in their hearts.

Properly translated as in the ESV and NASB, these verses read, "Are you bound to a wife? Do not seek to be free. Are you free (luō) from a wife? Do not seek a wife. But if you do marry, you have not sinned" (1 Corinthians 7:27-28a, ESV and NASB). As we see in these two translations, Paul is speaking to those married and those who are divorced and have remarried. Paul encouraged married individuals to stay married; Paul also spoke to the divorced person, assuring them that if they marry, they have not sinned. Paul's words free a divorced person for remarriage.

We are called by the word of God into the process of letting go of the boulder of misuse of the Scriptures. We are forgiven, freed, restored by the word of God from all aspects of our past life including but certainly not limited to divorce. Redemption is worked by God in the context of our brokenness, not apart from it.

BOULDER TWO: CONTROL

Letting go of the control boulder can be a big stumbling block for many people. We, quite likely, have felt out of control when our home was being disrupted. We attempt to try to make sense of chaos by gripping tightly to those aspects of life we can control. The control boulder includes futile attempts to make life neat and tidy. Life is not a smooth, straight path. Life is a journey, that today, living in redemption's freedom, I call a beautiful mess.

Attempting to control our past, present and future is a burden we are encouraged to lay down at the feet of Jesus and follow him, freed to live. I recall a picture of Jesus hanging on the wall of my church. Jesus had tender eyes that seemed to look at me regardless of my place in the room. His golden-brown hair flowed freely and His arms reached out inviting me to Himself. I never felt a desire to place my messes or my life into those arms as I believed they only invited perfection.

The following vivid image of Christ is more accurate in my particular story. I imagine Jesus, weeping for me, with me as I place the boulders of control on the dusty road (see *The Rock Speaks*, Cindy Steinbeck, Concordia Publishing House, 2016) His tears flow freely for my family, my former spouse, and for all who have been wounded by divorce. As He motions me to follow Him, I see a big scar on His hand and I shudder at the thought of a nail piercing the hands of this gentle man. Jesus turns His body and begins walking, leading me down a path unknown; I follow seeing only His back.

Jesus deliberately walks away from my control boulders and they stay in the place where I set them at His feet just moments before. The image of those boulders gets smaller and smaller when I glance back. As I follow Jesus on this unknown path, at times I want to turn around and run back to grab my control boulders. They are far more familiar, comfortable and comforting than this unknown journey. Jesus keeps walking and so I follow, surprisingly not out of control but feeling comforted that He is in control. His kindness encourages me to keep pace. The burden

He asks me to bear is light in comparison to the boulders I've left behind. I find myself trusting that He carried my brokenness in His life, in his death on the cross, and left it in the stinky grave.

I realize that Jesus is leading me down the path of hope and healing, a path of resurrection and restoration. Jesus pauses in a vineyard to say, "I am the vine; you are the branch. Abide in me" (see John 15:4-5). He encourages me to understand that my dwelling place is His very life, a place of safety, energy and healing. He helps me release my boulders of control, making space for His life to fill a deep void. He frees to live and breathe. I want intimacy with Him, even more intimacy than I'm experiencing with Him at this very moment. I want and need a safe place to grieve my loss and express my need to be loved and heard. This is the picture of Jesus that invites me to continue to release my boulders of control.

Boulders of control we also need to recognize and release are the boulders others carry and try to place on us. Coming to grips with the fact that other people attempt to control our past, present, or future is critical to the process of letting go. While perhaps done with innocent intentions, their boulders of control can cause further, deeper injury and pain. The following story is one painful experience where a person attempted to control my life.

I had concluded a well-received presentation to a group of ladies. I packed my car for my trip home and decided I would be wise to use the restroom prior to getting on the road. I proceeded back into the building. When I exited the restroom into the dark hallway a man stopped me. We hadn't been introduced, but I recognized that he was one of the pastors of the church. He had been in attendance at my presentation. I stepped into the light, surprised at his approach and demeanor. He said, "I'd like to ask you a question, is that ok?" I said, "yes." He asked, "Have you ever thought about reconciling with your ex?" I answered, "Yes, of course." He proceeded to tell me that I needed to reconcile and that doing so would be such a great witness to the church. He assured me that my former spouse had changed.

My heart was racing at the impromptu meeting. I asked, "Do you know him?" He said, "No, not really." I asked, "How do you know he has changed?" He said, "________________ told me he has changed." I knew the person he was referring to and was shaken to know that they had been discussing my life with little knowledge of what took place in the privacy of our home. After a few words to try to explain my life choices, I gained composure, realizing nothing I could say would make any difference. I quickly excused myself, got into my car and drove away.

In this example we see one control boulder, the misuse of an individual's position as a religious leader, being used to attempt to control a human being. My transparent presentation moments before had revealed my brokenness and journey into Christ mercy for hope and healing. He did not know my heart. In fact, my safety and my heart were not important to him. Guarding the institution of marriage and me being an example were his only goals. This experience taught me to practice placing healthy boundaries around myself so that people wouldn't be given an opportunity to try to use their boulders of control against me.

BOULDER THREE: FEAR

Fear is a very heavy boulder God's word calls us to lay at the feet of Jesus and follow Him into hope and healing. We may have become frozen in fear that blocks growth. Fear of the past or the future winds itself through the fabric of one's being making it exceptionally challenging, if not impossible, to live in the present.

The boulders of fear that create major stumbling blocks are abundant. For some the fear of being alone means they get involved in an intimate relationship quickly without feeling the pain and healing from the previous relationship. For others, fear leads to isolation and a vow to never love or be loved again. Other fears include a fear of failure, fear of what others might think, fear of intimacy, fear of vulnerability. Some dread being alone, others dread being with people, some fear both. Jesus calls us to follow him as he guides us into finding safe places in which to let go of our fear boulders.

Naming and letting go of one boulder at a time gives us opportunity to learn the beauty of letting go. This long-term process leads to growth and maturity, a critical aspect of living in the present. Like Mary, Martha, and Lazarus, we are called to rely on Christ's word and work to raise us up in the process of letting go. We are called to rely on one another to take off the clothes of death that bind us. Letting go involves feeling pain, so please continue on with me as we explore the critical step of feeling pain as God works redemption through divorce.

CHAPTER 9

Pain

God created feelings, and God created human beings to feel feelings. Feeling gives us opportunity to live life fully alive. We have choices. We are invited to cherish God's creative gift and journey more fully into understanding that the gift of feeling feelings reveals much about His heart. We also have the distinct choice and ability to flee from feeling. To live life fully alive we must choose curiosity and leaning into feeling feelings. Our focus will be the feeling of pain as it relates to broken hearts and divorce, understanding that many emotions like sadness, anger, or fear could be substituted for feeling pain.

God works through pain to call us into a deeper relationship with Himself. We cry out, "We want to be free of pain, why can't we live life with no pain?" Pain indicates that something is wrong and is often connected to relationships with people.

Relationships with others have likely caused great pain in our very real, human pilgrimage on this earth. Relationships also have the profound potential to usher us along in the journey of hope and healing. We return to the story of the very first relationship as we look into feeling pain.

God breathed His breath into Adam, creating life and longing for relationship. God further expressed His magnificent creation of human beings by giving Adam a partner and work, both designed to fulfill his longing for aliveness. Adam's wife and work were not given to replace his longing for life but rather designed to complement it while mirroring his relationship with God. Adam's aliveness was expressed fully in his relationship with God as well as in and through his relationship with his wife and his work.

Sadly, Adam and Eve sought life and aliveness where it could not be found. They decided that there must be more to the life God had given to them and that God was simply, selfishly hiding something about life from them. Through one act of disobedience growing from the temptation to know more, death entered God's perfectly designed creation. Adam and Eve certainly knew a lot more after doing exactly what God had commanded them not to do. Among many other things, including journeying toward their own death, they learned that they would feel the pain of their wrong.

Adam and Eve turned God's gifts and opportunity for worship into an act of disobedience. This act brought punishment and death into this world. God's design went terribly awry the day Adam and Eve chose to express themselves in a way contrary to God's design and command. Their disobedience did not change God; their disobedience changed them. God's desire for life-giving relationship did not end. Rather, God continued to pursue Adam and Eve to give them life in relationship. God promised redemption in the life of His son; their lives would need to be lived in that promise and hope. Life, from that point in history, would include the pain of brokenness. They had choices. They could run and try to hide from pain or live by faith and trust in God's promise of life in the midst of pain.

Brokenness of the human heart and death of the human body were two aspects of that one act of disobedience. Adam and Eve's relationship with God was forever changed that moment of that day. Brokenness led to feeling fear and hiding as well as feeling shame and blaming. They lied, they pointed fingers, and they felt despair on that one day. Pain upon pain resulted. Shortly thereafter in the Scriptures we read about murder and a long list of brokenness, including abusing human life and misusing sex. In an attempt to mask the pain of deep brokenness, people sought relief from pain where it could not be found.

FEELING PAIN

Can we feel pain? Do we medicate our pain and if so, how? Have we become numb to pain thereby becoming numb to life? Can we take the courage to identify our pain and allow God to work through it? I am not a clinical expert in this topic but I certainly have gained wisdom from a life-long history of running from feeling pain. I choose to acknowledge pain and I choose to lean into pain. I choose to identify ways I medicate my pain. I choose to feel, even though it is scary because I know that avoiding pain (or other emotions I may have identified as negative) is not living life alive.

Authors Paul Brand and Phillip Yancey (*The Gift of Pain, Zondervan, 1997)* believe that pain is a gift from God to be treasured. Brand's lifelong work as a physician was spent caring for people with leprosy. Among other things, leprosy is a disease in which people feel no pain. Observing people who cannot feel pain fueled his understanding that pain and feeling pain is a necessary part of living in this world. Pain is a symptom alerting us that something is wrong. If we cannot feel pain, we place ourselves in grave danger.

A person suffering from physical pain may identify the pain and seek diagnosis by a physician. Western culture and Western medicine often separate human life into compartments and specialties, to great detriment of human life. Eastern culture views a human being as a whole being with heart and soul as the center of life. Thankfully, there is movement in our Western world back toward treating the person as a whole being. Physical pain is intimately connected to mental, emotional and spiritual pain. We must understand that when one aspect of a human's life is wounded and in pain, all parts of his or her being suffers.

Integrating the whole being is necessary to living fully alive in this world. Henry Cloud, in his masterfully written book

Integrity (Harper-Collins, 2006) guides the reader in the journey of integrating one's entire being. His observation is that life contains two paths, one healthy, the other unhealthy—integration or disintegration. Disintegration takes place through compartmentalizing life that leads to breakdown of the being. Integration welcomes feeling feelings in general, and feeling pain specifically and is intimately connected to our inner being. Those not connected to their inner being often run from living life as one means to avoid pain.

Running from danger is healthy and necessary in crisis. Here are a few examples: fleeing when gun shots are fired, running away from a bear or swimming away from a shark, driving away from a fire, fighting off sexual assault. If we are unable to physically flee from imminent danger, fleeing takes place in the mind. God designed us this way so that we can protect ourselves in the midst of crisis. We were not created to stay in the fleeing mode for the long term.

God designed us to mentally, emotionally, physically, and spiritually discern crisis after it has passed. We must do so with safe human beings with whom we can be vulnerable. We must process pain and associated emotions such as sadness, guilt, shame, or fear. If we don't have opportunity to process pain, we internalize it and keep it as though the crisis were still present. Shame and silence set in when we don't voice our pain or even have a safe environment in which to do so. Without a place to discern our pain we often numb our pain through a vast array of means that are likely to lead to addiction in various forms.

Numbing pain is an unhealthy survival tactic, one in which life in its fullness cannot be lived.

Running from internal pain led me to seek relationships that diverted my attention away from my pain. I set out, innocently and lovingly, with the desire to help other people who were in pain. I did not know that I didn't have the skills to deal with the complex issues I faced or we faced. These relationships, that I was trying to use to get out of pain, led to greater pain.

My marriage relationship included many forms of running from pain, including running from the pain associated with the cycle of domestic violence. Periods of calm were present until something would stimulate an angry outburst. Outbursts led to promises to be better, to do better. Making up provided great feelings of relief and hope until the next outburst took place. I ignored and avoided feeling pain by engaging in intense work to make me and our relationship better. I also embarked on furthering my education. My spouse numbed the pain through a variety of means. Despair reigned. Isolation and fear dominated life.

Asking for help allowed me to begin making sense of the pain I couldn't or didn't want to feel. Facing the pain led to feeling the pain, and that led to saying "ouch" when I hurt. Facing pain led to more pain, the pain of separation and divorce. Divorce brought the freedom to process and feel pain from the context of healthy relationships.

God worked and continues to work through pain to bring life. As I mentioned previously, I never expected to be divorced or a divorce statistic, but I always longed to live life fully as a human being. God has worked aliveness in my life, through pain. God has worked hope and healing in the lives of many I've spoken with. I've learned, since voicing my pain and then telling some of my story, that I have a lot in common with many human beings.

PAINFUL REDEMPTION STORIES

As I've told my own very human story, many people have shared their stories with me. Their stories reflect redemption through their tragedy as well as the pain they've endured at the mercy of those flailing about in a hopeless attempt to find life through hurting others. I've observed that every human thought or action is either an act of redemption, life breeding life, or a futile attempt at fulfilling a God-designed longing for life. I chose the word futile carefully—it means fruitless, ineffective, to no avail, barren, and hopeless.

Redemption is at work when a person cries out for help and says, "no more" to hurtful relationships. Redemption's work is evident in these pain-filled stories. Some women remain in great pain and others have navigated their way from despair to hope. These stories are from women who had the courage to speak with me about their pain after I shared pieces of my story. Men experience the same types of pain and also need a safe place in which they can share their stories.

- A woman was one of three daughters. Her father chose her as the one he would sexually assault. As a woman she lived a troubled life. She married an abusive man and when she divorced him, she was shamed by her parents.

- A woman was assaulted and raped at 7 years old. Her mother told her it was her fault. She was repeatedly told that she sought it out and was blamed for the abuse.
- A woman was married to a respected church leader. Their children were conceived of rape. She divorced him and was shamed by him as well as the people in their church.
- A woman lived silently in a home filled with anger and rage. Her spouse was charming to everyone else and even to her in public but violent at home. No one would believe her story, but she had the courage to flee and build loving relationships with safe people.
- A woman is regularly beaten with a baseball bat but doesn't leave because she has nowhere to go.
- A woman lived for fifty-four years in an abusive marriage and her spouse died. She cried out that grieving this loss is very different than the experience of grief of her friends who lived in a loving marriage.
- A woman lived an emotionally abusive marriage—no physical violence took place in her home. Words were twisted to flee from the real issues. She was made to feel inept and stupid while being told "I love you."
- A woman married and eventually divorced an abusive spouse. Her parents and community shamed her into remarrying him. She divorced him a second time

because of continued domestic violence and doesn't continue her relationship with her parents or the church community.

- A woman was verbally abused by her mother throughout her childhood. She carried her mom's abusive words into adulthood and marriage.
- A teenaged girl was brutally raped and left for dead. She recovered from the physical wounds but carries the shame of rape into all aspects of her life.
- A woman told graphic stories of emotional, physical and verbal abuse to her minister. He told her the facts weren't enough to leave the marriage and divorce her spouse because "God hates divorce."
- A grieving mother shared that her daughter's abusive marriage ended when her daughter was murdered by her son-in-law.
- Many, many people have told stories of over eating, under eating, cutting, drug and alcohol abuse in order to numb pain as well as many stories of general lack of self-care.

We cry out in pain, "Good Lord, have mercy!" As we can see from these stories, and there are many more untold, pain abounds in a religious culture where life may be preached but is hardly practiced. Silence is expected under the guise of submission. Pain turns into a dull ache and the God-designed longing for life fades into an unrecognizable part of unspeakable pain. If life is lived in silence bred by constant fear or danger, the God-designed longing for freedom can be swallowed up by depression. Depression breeds despair. Do we dare hope for healing?

HOPE IN THE MIDST OF PAIN

Hope and healing shatter despair just as light shatters darkness. Light breeds more light, light breeds hope, and hope breeds freedom. Light also breeds honesty. Speaking the truth in love is a critical aspect of finding hope in the midst of pain. Light brings God's redemptive work into life and urges us to live life as fully alive human beings. Voicing our pain as we feel our pain is critical as we grow, understanding that pain is very personal. We are to use wisdom as we share our pain, knowing that some will not cherish us as human beings, but rather use our pain against us. When I share stories, I am careful to only share stories where much healing has taken place and not re-open wounds.

I chose a Christian therapist, a woman's shelter, a divorce recovery group, and a few trusted friends as safe places to allow hope to work in me. Feeling hope took time because denial of pain, despair and depression were so prevalent and powerful. Despair and depression thrive in silence and silence fosters shame.

In great hope, in the midst of feeling pain, we trust that Christ's life wins. The enemies of Christ's victory cannot and do not win where truth prevails. The truth of Christ's victory wins; redemption through pain wins; redemption through divorce wins. God's redemption through divorce brings hope in the midst of pain. His work in us helps us discern our stories as He works redemption and healing in and through our particular life story. God's work in us is painful as He wakes up the dead parts of our being, but it is healthy pain. He works through our pain and through our stories to bring redemption hope to others.

God's final act of redemption for us will be the day He calls us to be face to face with Him. We trust that His redemptive work, either softening or hardening the hearts, of those who have hurt us has been taking place. We trust that He has worked through our divorce both in us and in the one we have divorced. We trust that He continues to work through our divorce to bring His story of redemption to life in us and through us.

Until we meet Christ face to face where there will be no more pain or tears or sadness, we welcome His redemptive, freeing work in our lives. Perfectly imperfect, our human life has been redeemed in Christ's perfect life, for life here and for all eternity. We are freed to be ourselves, to seek a life of safety and peace. We are free to feel pain, we are free to feel hope and experience healing.

CHAPTER 10

Living Forgiveness

Forgiveness—what do we do with this word, this concept from the context of our broken stories? How do we live forgiveness? How do we practice forgiveness in our lives? What does forgiveness mean? Forgiveness is an action, forgiveness is "to cancel a debt, to pardon, to give up resentment or the right to retaliation" (Merriam-Webster.com). We've already given up a lot and we have to give up more? Forgiveness is not simply a concept, forgiveness is a way of life, where the rubber hits the road in life.

Prior to discussing the practice of forgiveness and canceling a debt, we must understand the complexities of debt. Debt is something a person owes me or something I owe him. In a positive sense, we use the phrase, "I owe you a debt of gratitude," meaning, I am so thankful for what you have done for me, I express to you that I owe you something like my eternal thanks in return. In another sense, if I've taken out a loan, I owe a debt. I was likely required to sign a note of repayment in exchange for the loan.

Canceling these two types of debt is common and easy. In the first instance, the giver may reply, "It was my honor, you don't owe me anything" in an attempt to cancel the debt he feels he owes. In the second instance, the one who issued the loan may choose to cancel the debt, tear up the note of repayment and forgive the debt.

DEBT

What is debt in our very real, raw, painful stories? We must be transparently honest about the debt owed to us in order to step into forgiveness. Debt takes the form of wounds caused by people we love or have loved or with whom we have been in relationship. Our list of wounds may include physical pain, sexual trauma, emotional injury, spiritual injury, soul-based or spirit-based wounds. A broken heart and heartache are a debt owed. Years of lost time is a debt owed. Debt takes the form of vivid memories that may or may not fade with time. Debt multiplies when an offender will not take responsibility for his hurtful actions. Debt may be owed to us by a person who has died, prior to any sort of canceling the debt taking place. This adds a painfully complex dynamic to grieving loss.

Debt is owed to us. Ignoring or making light of the debt owed to us hampers forgiveness, so we take time to name it, specifically. Speak it aloud. Write out the debt. Feel the pain of the debt. Grieve losses. Cry the debt out to God, trusting that God knows our hearts and receives our cry. We can choose to hold on to the debt and work with all our might to force someone to repay what they owe us. We can choose to spend huge amounts of mental energy trying to figure out ways to impose repayment on another in hope of replacing the losses we've faced. When they fail to repay, and they will fail, old wounds are reopened, adding debt to debt.

An important aspect on the journey of forgiveness is asking ourselves questions. Can I ever, realistically, collect the debt owed? What do I want? What do I need? How can my heart be settled? How do deep wounds heal? What is best for me and for my family? Can I release the debt owed and maintain my composure or dignity? Can I forgive? These questions guide our journey more deeply into forgiveness.

FORGIVENESS

Forgiveness involves a choice to release debt. We choose to cancel the debt. Canceling debt is the healthy course of action, the one and only path that settles and heals our hearts. We've written down the debt owed and we tear up the note of repayment. Rejecting the alternative, to hold on tightly, we release. We let go. We forgive because we've been forgiven by Christ who lives alive in us, and we live alive in Christ. Christ is the master forgiver. Christ coaxes us, calls us to release debt.

Forgiveness flows from our hearts, not because of someone's apology and not withheld based upon a lack of genuine repentance. Canceling debt emanates from our being, not to let someone off the hook for wrong doing, but because it is God's job to hold others accountable. When we are unable to muster the desire or courage to forgive from our heart, we cry out to God to give us strength to forgive.

Forgiveness may never take place in an encounter with an offender because that may not be safe. If it is safe and an offender has truly taken responsibility for their actions, canceling the debt may take place by speaking forgiveness directly to them. Some relationships can be rebuilt on the foundation of forgiveness; others cannot. In many cases, both parties are called to mutually forgive one another. While all cases are unique, the common factor is that forgiving frees the heart.

"Forgive and forget" is a dangerous mantra often attached to scriptural truth. We make unsuccessful attempts to try to forget. God never suggests or asks that of human beings. He created the human brain to remember. We cannot and should not forget. We learn to embrace remembering from the context of choosing to forgive. Memories are a valuable tool, created by God to assist us in the process of living life. We also remember so we don't make the same choices that cause pain rather than breed life.

Scripture declares that God chooses to "remember our sins no more" (see Jeremiah 31:34, Hebrews 8:12, 10:17). King David sings out, "For as high as the heavens are above the earth, so great is his steadfast love toward those who fear him; as far as the east is from the west, so far does he remove our transgressions from us," (Psalm 103:11-12). God removes sin, choosing to forgive sin and not use the debt we owe him against us.

My vineyard has provided a resting place for the burdens I have carried because of the sins of others against me as well as my own sin and brokenness. Row 124 is a place in the middle of a field of grapevines. It is a place that holds many rocks, all representing choices I, and many others who have journeyed to 124, have made to release debt from our being. The large pile of rocks in row 124 represent a painful remembering and an intentional leaving of boulders at the feet of Christ, the True Vine.

Forgiveness is a process like walking a mile to row 124 with a boulder in hand with the intention of letting go. Remembering and visualizing the offenses in the boulder is an intentional way of allowing release to take place. The exercise of forgiveness doesn't take place in one quick, easy step. Forgiveness is a conscious, recurring effort to let go.

Forgiveness of self and others is a process and a practice rooted in our Lord's call to pray, "Our Father in heaven, hallowed be your name. Your kingdom come, your will be done, on earth as it is in heaven. Give us this day our daily bread, and forgive us our debts, as we also have forgiven our debtors. And lead us not into temptation, but deliver us from evil," (Matthew 6:9-13). This prayer challenges us to trust what Jesus knew: one of the greatest temptations we will ever face is to choose to hold tightly to the debt others owe us. He knew the human heart and its unhealthy desire to hold on to debt. After being delivered and freed, we are tempted to hold on to the wrong another has done. Christ continued with these wake-up words, "For if you forgive others their trespasses, your heavenly Father will also forgive you, but if you do not forgive others their trespasses, neither will your Father forgive your trespasses," (Matthew 6:14-15).

We have been forgiven by Christ; we are called to forgive those who have sinned against us, with our whole heart and being. Peter wondered aloud to Christ, how many times must I forgive? Jesus' answered, infinity! Impossible? In Christ, all things are possible (see Matthew 18:21-22, Matthew 19:26). Forgiveness is the path to life, hope, and healing Christ won for us.

We must make sure we don't misunderstand forgiveness as that would lead us down a path of confusion and despair. Forgiveness means letting go but it does not mean placing ourselves in situations where another has opportunity to repeatedly hurt us. Scripture is clear, we are to guard our hearts and lives as valuable human beings created by God for living life. Scripture contains great wisdom regarding relationships and guarding our hearts. Here is one example from Proverbs, "Make no friendship with a man given to anger, nor go with a wrathful man," (Proverbs 22:24). King David fled from danger on many occasions rather than allowing Saul or other enemies to hurt or kill him (see 1 Samuel 21, 1 Samuel 27, 2 Samuel 15).

Forgiveness can be a onetime event, but most often forgiveness takes time. Here are a few examples from my life story. I'm often surprised and caught off guard by the forgiveness process. The surprise usually follows on the heels of thinking,

"I've arrived, I'm finally here at the place of forgiving my former spouse." Soon after, here becomes a place of great struggle to forgive, again. The challenge to continue to forgive comes when memories of painful experiences arise or memories of good times come to mind or our children are hurt or significant dates pass. All of the above and more trigger the need to practice the difficult task of forgiving.

Self-doubt is another aspect of my divorce that catches me off guard and gives me plenty of opportunity to forgive myself. I interrogate myself with seemingly endless questions. "Did I work hard enough?" "What did I do wrong?" "Why couldn't I save our marriage?" These harsh, painful thoughts indicate my continued need to allow Christ's forgiveness to permeate my being. I must allow God's word to cancel the debt I believe I owe me. I must choose to tear up the note and release the debt I hold against myself.

REDEMPTION

Redeem means "to purchase or buy back, to free from captivity by payment of a ransom, the action of regaining or gaining possession of something in exchange for payment" (Merriam-Webster.com). Scripture points to one Redeemer who, through his blood, bought us back with His life. Christ freed us from captivity. The Apostle Paul declared, "In Him we have redemption through his blood, the forgiveness of our trespasses, according to the riches of

His grace, which He lavished upon us, in all wisdom and insight," (Ephesians 1:7-8).

The young man on my winery patio on that cold January day made the profound statement, "God working redemption through divorce." Over the phone line a week later I asked, "Why did you say "redemption through divorce?" These words flowed from his heart: "I said it because I believe the theme of all Scripture is redemption." My heart woke up with God's word from him as he continued to speak of redemption. He didn't need to go into great detail about the divorce of his parents. He didn't tell me how, what, and why, or who was at fault. He spoke of their broken hearts and their inability to hear and receive mercy because they divorced. Each had remarried and carried the guilt of divorce and remarriage because of the misuse of Scripture. As their son, he hungered for them to hear Jesus' mercy and to receive that mercy so their hearts could be freed in the life of Christ, the one who works redemption through divorce.

REDEMPTION AND FORGIVENESS

Redeem and forgive both mean the clearing of a debt. Redemption and forgiveness are intimate partners flowing from a loving Savior who paid the ultimate ransom with His very life. One example of redemption freedom is Jesus' loud cry from the cross, "Father, forgive (aphiemi) them for they know not what they do," (Luke 23:34). From the depth of His being, upon completion of redemption, Christ breathed His last breath and He died (see

Mark 15:37). This redemption cry led to the tomb, through death, and into resurrected life. Christ worked then and Christ continues His resurrected, redemptive, and forgiving work for all time.

Christ has redeemed and forgiven us, pursuing us for an eternal relationship with Him today, now. His redemption and forgiveness loose us from all that would bind us and keep us from living life. Christ's redemption and forgiveness permeate every aspect of our being, cleansing us and making us whole. We cry out in a loud voice too, "Christ, forgive them for they don't know what they have done to us," and "Father, forgive me, for not knowing then what I know now, for any hardness in my heart, for any debt against me I hold, and for the things I've left undone." With that cry, we give up, we release any debt owed to us as well as the bonds of our self-accusation. Flowing from our redemption cry is the cry of hope, leading to joy even in the midst of pain.

God's work of redemption and forgiveness has the power to touch the hearts of those who have caused great offense by dealing treacherously or with violence against another human being. Offenders may be led to cry out to God and to the one they offended, "please forgive me for the damage I have done." The offender must come to grips with the fact that he or she may not be safe and that the person or persons they violated may never trust them. They can rest knowing that God's forgiveness is for them but they may never hear, "I forgive you" from the one they offended. They must give up too. They must give up the right to be in the presence of those they have violated. Sadly, many violators speak "I'm sorry" with their mouths, but in their hearts construe only selfish or evil intentions. Only God knows their hearts and, I repeat, those who have been violated must protect their lives and those they love from danger.

Christ's desire for wholeness is for all people and is reflected in His sacrificial love. He takes our burdens and brokenness into His life. He swallows up death with resurrection life. His call to follow Him is a redemption call, a forgiveness call. We rise up with Him, in His life, to resurrection living. We follow Him, redeemed and forgiven, whole and holy because of His life for us and in us. In His great wisdom as He works for us and in us. He also works redemption through us in the lives of others. Shame fades, making room for courageous story telling about how redemption and forgiveness has permeated our being.

Grasping hold of and clinging tightly to mercy "for me" gives us profound opportunity to trust God at His word, in the midst of our broken stories. We receive as God cancels the debt we owe Him. We beg God to remove bitterness, anger, spite, revenge, a desire for retaliation, and any other aspect of holding on to the debt others owe us. We choose to cancel debts owed and live in mercy toward ourselves and toward others through redemption and forgiveness in Christ.

CONCLUSION

Redemption Through Divorce is filled with stories. There are many stories of broken hearts and the impact of that brokenness on heart, soul, mind, body, and spirit of individual human beings. I've also woven into my work the way in which misuse of God's word places people further into despair and bondage. The most important stories on which to focus and meditate are the stories of Christ's redemption work in broken hearts creating hope and healing. God's word calls us into these powerful stories and allow them to be our stories.

The journey into redemption's healing is a life-long process. Redemption hope and healing is a powerful call on our lives, urging us to grow. As we grow, we will more and more clearly see God's work through our life experiences. I pray that redemption hope rings loudly for you as it has for me. I'm honored to have walked with you during your time reading and processing these words from my heart. Please, when you're in Paso Robles, CA stop by to say hi and share a few stories. Take a Jeep ride with me to hear more about my grape vines and Christ's work through them. We can stop at row 124 if you'd like to place a boulder in the vines. We can laugh and cry together as we continue to grow in hope and healing.

Visit my website www.voiceinthevineyard.org and look at the photos and videos taken in my vineyard. These pictures and videos speak volumes about the process of growing and healing. Jot down the date you first look at the photos and read this book. Return to *Redemption Through Divorce* at yearly intervals and make note of the ways in which you've grown and healed.

May God continue to create life in your being to bring hope and healing. May God continue to breathe life into your being to give you the courage to receive His redemption work through forgiveness, mercy, and grace. May you have courage to be an agent of redemption and forgiveness in the lives of others as God works through your brokenness to touch lives with hope. Christ's life, His word, and His breath give us courage as He works redemption *through* divorce. God will continue to pursue, to speak life, and breathe life in you because He wants an intimate relationship with you. He created you to live life fully in Him.

One last note, play, and rejoice. If you don't know how, watch children play and play with them. Let them teach you how to pause, create, live in the moment to experience pure joy at little things. Smell flowers and watch the sun rise and the sun set.

Watch the moon and the stars with wide-eyed wonder. Listen to music, dance, and sing. Little by little the hope and healing in Christ we've discussed in these pages will become part of the fabric of your being. Please, reach out for help to appropriate people if you find yourself feeling hopeless—your life is a gift.

—With love, Cindy

Made in the USA
Monee, IL
13 March 2025

13492274R00080